Endorsements
Life-Changing Verses

Life-Changing Verses is the kind of book that God can use to reach into the deepest places of your heart. Carlton Arnold writes with warmth, insight, and a profound understanding not only of God's Word but also the way people think, feel, and live. Taking time each day to read a short chapter from this wonderful book can transform your life!"

> *Dr. Steven Rummage*
> *Senior Pastor*
> *Visiting Professor of Preaching*
> *Southeastern Baptist Theological*
> *Seminary*
> *Bell Shoals Baptist Church*
> *Brandon, FL*

Having been the recipient of *Life-Changing Verses*, I have been deeply impressed with the manner in which the Author has taken familiar and not so familiar verses of Scripture and opened them to an explosion of meaning and application. His faithfulness to the context and Biblical Doctrine has made the study exciting. I am also impressed with his challenge in the book for the reader to apply the message to his or her daily life.

> *Dr. Marion Beaver*
> *Seniors Pastor*
> *First Baptist Church*
> *Lithia Springs, GA*

It has been my honor to know Carlton Arnold as a volunteer church member and as a staff person. In both situations, Carlton is a man who loves the Word of God and is passionate about teaching the Bible. With experience and compassion he is a faithful mentor to men, young and old, who want to know more of God's Word and apply biblical principles to their life. In Psalm 89:1 David wrote, "I will sing about the Lord's faithful love forever; I will proclaim Your faithfulness to all generations with my mouth." Carlton "sings" through his teaching about God's love to young and old.

> *Dr. Bob Jolly, Pastor*
> *First Baptist Church*
> *Cumming, GA*

My good friend and brother in Christ, Carlton Arnold, has been given a unique gift to impart God's Word in a way that is pertinent, personal and crystal clear, so that I know God is speaking to me. These are words with the power to change one's life, and indeed they have done so with mine.

Walter L. (Lou) Meier III, M.D.

LIFE CHANGING VERSES

VOLUME 2

Carlton Lee Arnold

WestBow
PRESS
A DIVISION OF THOMAS NELSON

WestBow Press books may be ordered through booksellers or by contacting:

WestBow Press
A Division of Thomas Nelson
1663 Liberty Drive
Bloomington, IN 47403
www.westbowpress.com
1-(866) 928-1240

Because of the dynamic nature of the Internet, any web addresses or links contained in this book may have changed since publication and may no longer be valid. The views expressed in this work are solely those of the author and do not necessarily reflect the views of the publisher, and the publisher hereby disclaims any responsibility for them.

Any people depicted in stock imagery provided by Thinkstock are models, and such images are being used for illustrative purposes only.

Certain stock imagery © Thinkstock.

NIV – New International Version
Scripture taken from the Holy Bible, New International Version®. Copyright © 1973, 1978, 1984 Biblica. Used by permission of Zondervan. All rights reserved.

ISBN: 978-1-4497-8946-6 (sc)
ISBN: 978-1-4497-8947-3 (hc)
ISBN: 978-1-4497-8945-9 (e)

Library of Congress Control Number: 2013905435

Printed in the United States of America.

WestBow Press rev. date: 4/1/2013

Shout for joy to the Lord,
all the earth.
Worship the Lord
with gladness;
Come before him
with joyful songs.

OTHER WORKS BY THE AUTHOR

*L*IFE-*CHANGING VERSES, VOLUME 1,* WAS published in 2012. This is the second volume of a planned four volume set of *Life-Changing Verses.* You will find that there are no repeated verses or chapters. Each set of verses are unique to the entire set of the four Volumes. Volume 3 is scheduled to be published in November, 2013.

While teaching the two year through the Bible class, my son took it upon himself to digitally record each class. He transcribed these notes verbatim. They are available at www.allarnold.com. You are encouraged to visit the site to read about the Old Testament and the New Testament, especially about God's story in both testaments. If you have any questions or comments, please let me know at carlton47@gmail.com.

In another two year class, a class member took it upon himself to video tape each lesson and transfer them to DVD. Each lesson is available for a nominal fee. Note: there is a special seven week study of the book of Revelation that has been taught in several Bible Study classes. For more information, access my email: carltonlcv@gmail.com.

There are numerous other classes originated by the author to help Christians understand their life in Christ.

These classes include: *Holy Spirit, Prayer,* and *What is Discipleship?*

Life-Changing Verses

Volume 2

Encouragement for the Believer

to Apply God's Word with Conviction

To my wife, D'Ette,

To my son, Eric,

To my daughter, Erin, and

To my other daughter, Ginger

What an interesting road we have traveled together.

I would not change a thing!

I have been crucified with Christ

and I no longer live,

but Christ lives in me.

The life I live in the body,

I live by faith in the Son of God,

who loved me and gave himself for me.

Galatians 2:20

CONTENTS

FOREWORD

As a HOSPICE CHAPLAIN, I often feel a sense of helplessness in the face of suffering and death. So often patients and families tell me, "I don't know what I would do without the Lord." In this world of suffering there is nothing we need more than a personal relationship with Jesus Christ.

Last year, Blaine Cooper, a member of First Baptist Church of Cumming, Georgia, introduced me to Carlton Arnold. I had the joy of caring for Blaine's mother as her hospice chaplain. Blaine had been blessed by Carlton's *Life-Changing Verses* and felt the leading by the Holy Spirit to connect me with Carlton's reflections. I am so glad that she did!

My favorite verse in Scripture is Psalm 16:11: "You make known to me the path of life; you will fill me with joy in your presence, with eternal pleasures at your right hand." As I read Carlton's devotions, I am brought into God's presence. He writes in ways that bring me joy. I feel the Holy Spirit speaking through his words which are full of practical advice. However, if you are looking for soft, comforting words—look elsewhere. Carlton will encourage you, but he is quick to challenge you to live the life that God has always wanted you to live.

I laughed when I learned that Carlton's favorite verse is Philippians 1:6: "Being confident of this, that he who began a good work in you will carry it on to completion until the day of Christ Jesus." As you might know, Philippians is Paul's book of joy. When we enter into God's presence we experience God's joy and when we allow Him to change us, He changes us into the people He always wanted us to become.

I challenge you to experience the Holy Spirit's power through reading

Life- Changing Verses. I'm confident, as you listen to Carlton's heartfelt words, that God will continue his good work in you and bring you His joy.

Rev. Scott Uzzel; M.Div., BCC
Georgia Hospice
2001 Professional Way; Suite 240
Woodstock, GA 30188

PREFACE

*L*IFE-*CHANGING* *VERSES* ARE A COMPILATION of my personal write-ups about selected verses from the Bible. Most write-ups are only one verse and some are well recognized while others are more obscure.

They were published on a weekly basis, and the audience has experienced continued growth over the years. I have been encouraged by many to format the *Life-Changing Verses* into book form so that others might find them helpful. This is Volume 2 and I plan to write two more. Volume 3 should be published in November, 2013.

These are not "soft" devotionals where you can say that you spent time with God. I am frank and candid about the current situation of the average Believer. This is based on over 35 years of Bible teaching with the last 14 years spent in teaching the Bible through seven times to classes that averaged over 75 people each Sunday.

My guiding principle was to encourage Christians to understand what the Bible says about being a Believer. My main objective for each Bible verse selected was to make real and practical application to a Believer's life. I experienced changes in my life while writing many of the *Life-Changing Verses*. I have a strong opinion that conviction will occur with every Believer. To God be the glory.

You will also find each *Life Changing Verse* helpful to get to know your Bible. I intentionally included the story surrounding the verse(s). Also, the way you think of your Christian life will be challenged.

For each chapter, I used the following Bible study technique:

Observation: What is the context of the verse; what is the story behind the verses

Interpretation: What is the meaning of the verses from a real life and spiritual perspective

Application: How do the verses enable you to grow in the grace and knowledge of God, Christ, and the Holy Spirit

Life-Change: Specific statements are provided that challenge how a person thinks about God. This is where the reader can experience a true life-change

Finally, a surprise to me was the use of these *Life-Changing Verses* in Bible Study classes. They are used to generate discussions about various topics. To help with the use of *Life-Changing Verses* for Bible study, I have included two indices in the back of the book to find topics to discuss. The first is a list of the Bible verses used and the second is a list by major topic.

Each *Life-Changing Verse* was written by the leading of the Holy Spirit for individual use. I pray that you will be challenged, convicted, and encouraged by each one. And from your reading these, I pray that there will be changes in your life that can be attributed to the power of God as administered by the Holy Spirit.

All writings are the thoughts of the author as prompted by the Holy Spirit. The writer's sole purpose was to see the hearts and minds of Believers directed toward God after reading *Life-Changing Verses*. May God and His Son, Jesus Christ, be honored through these writings.

All of the verses are quoted from the New International Version.

INTRODUCTION

You and I live in a world that is constantly calling for our attention. News of an event, which in previous decades we might have heard about on the 6 o'clock news, is now in the mainstream in minutes if not seconds after it occurs. We have instant access to any piece of information or news story or report we need or want, and at times this information seems to scream for our immediate attention.

Our phones, computers, tablets (and even friends!) are constantly in a state of, "have you heard?"; "have you seen"; "do you know?" And we are somehow made to feel out of touch or to feel less human, even if we don't know or don't answer or don't respond.

Into that world drops an email from Carlton every week that speaks to me and says, "Wait a second…are you focused on what really matters? Or are you simply trying to keep up in a race that someone else decided you should be in?

This book has come into your hands, and in a sense, it is asking you the same question; are you focused on what really matters? How would you answer that today? Is God speaking to you, into your stress, into your life? Life-Changing Verses can allow God to speak to you and your concerns for your day, your family, your career, and your life. They really are life-changing!

My Life-Changing Verses email usually seemed to arrive on the right day--a day that I needed to stop and listen to God. Often, they weren't read the day they hit the inbox, but a day or two days later. Even then, it seemed to consistently say what I needed to hear that day, and I praise God for that.

So, what are you focused on? Try using this book; the book you've taken enough time to read this far and let God work through the words of guidance, wisdom, and peace. Let Him show you what a day could be like when your focus is not on the noise of life, but on what truly makes life, life indeed.

I hope you enjoy this book as much as I have enjoyed reading Life-Changing Verses, and I hope it blesses you and encourages you the way it has me. I pray God works a life-change in you!

David Jernigan
Church Life Minister
Grace Chapel Church of Christ
Cumming, Georgia

1

GOD

IS NOT AN IMPERSONAL GOD!

> From one man he made every nation of men that they should inhabit the whole earth; and he determined the times set for them and the exact places where they should live. God did this so that men would seek him and perhaps reach out for him and find him, though he is not far from each one of us. 'For in him we live and move and have our being.' As some of your own poets have said, 'We are his offspring.'
>
> —ACTS 17:26-28

THESE VERSES MAKE A PLACE in Athens, Greece very famous. This is the location of Paul's sermon to the intellectuals of that city around A.D. 52. When Paul entered Athens, he saw that the Athenian people had all kinds of idols that they worshipped. They even had one that was dedicated to the "Unknown God" just in case they had overlooked a god in all of their idols. Paul was confronted by some of the people of Athens when he started discussing Jesus Christ. They asked him to explain his strange ideas about the God he was talking about. He proceeded to describe the God who they worshipped as the unknown god. During this explanation, Paul made the statements above. You can read the entire fascinating story in Acts 17:16-34.

During his explanation, Paul describes God as determining how long each person will live and where they will live. Now, I don't know about you, but these two actions by God are hard to comprehend in today's world. It's hard for us Believers to accept that God knows us so intimately that He determines when our death will be the best for His will to be done. Also, can you believe that God actually determined where you have lived, where you are living now, and where you will live in the future?

You see, there are a lot of people who believe that God created everything and then turned it over to "man" to do with it whatever he wants. To them, God is a hands-off God. He may be observing what we do on earth, but He never gets involved. This type of belief is called "deism." Deism is a religious or philosophical view of God and the world that describes God as Creator but stops there. In deism, the relationship between man and God is impersonal. God does not actively intervene in individual human affairs. Therefore, He would not be involved in when we die or where we live.

The problem with deism is that it does not accept miracles or revelations from God since God does not intervene in human history. With the huge push today to explain everything in natural or scientific terms, God is no longer a part of every day life. This is where some Believers are on the delicate edge of their belief. A Believer who has a hard time accepting miracles is leaning toward the religion of deism without being aware of it. Their God becomes impersonal. They have to live their lives with only what they know, with the strength they have, and with their own understanding of how things work. For example, a lot of Christians today trust themselves to get things done rather than trusting God. These Christians leave God to creating everything but cannot believe that He is intimately and deeply involved in their personal everyday lives. Read these verses again: God determines…!

Now, why does God do these two things: determine where we live and when we die? He knows the environment and the events that each of us needs to seek Him and find Him. My wife and I have lived in six different states during our marriage. I thought the first two were our choice. But now I know better. God knew where we should live! The remaining four states were clearly God-ordained, and we knew it. We can now see that those locations, with their unique environment and events, were exactly what we needed to know God better. Frankly, there were a couple of places that we would never have moved to in a million years. But, God determined where we should live for spiritual growth to occur in our family.

Finally, when you, as a Believer, accept God's personal relationship with you and His desire to be a real and active part of every second of your life, you will know your ultimate life purpose. As the verse above says, in Him you live, move, and exist! What an unbelievable (by worldly standards) aspect of living life! God has determined to be a personal God to you. The question is, "Do you let Him?"

2

YOUR LIFE
OFFER YOURSELF
CONTINUALLY TO GOD

Do not offer the parts of your body to sin, as instruments
of wickedness, but rather offer yourselves to God, as
those who have been brought from death to life; and
offer the parts of your body to him as instruments of
righteousness.

—ROMANS 6:13

MY WIFE WAS TAKING OUR new baby daughter to meet her grandparents.
It was a two-hour flight from Dallas, TX to Atlanta, GA. My wife
had bought brand-new clothes for the baby to be wearing when her parents
would see their granddaughter for the first time. My wife wanted her to be
as "cute" as she could be. She also was taking our three-year-old son with
her on the trip. The plane ride was a nightmare for her and the kids. By
the time her parents saw our baby daughter, all she had left to wear was a
diaper and a white t-shirt. She had spit up, messed up, drooled over, and
dirtied up all of the clothes my wife had carried with her. Fortunately, it
wasn't the clothes that the grandparents wanted to see. My wife did her
best to present our baby to her parents…the baby had other ideas.

What about the life of a Believer…YOU?! What do you do on a daily
basis to present yourself to our Heavenly Father, God? The verse above says

to offer yourself to God, and to do that with a specific thought in mind. That particular thought should occur in a Believer on a daily basis (if not hourly or even more frequently). The thought is this: you were "dead" and now you have been made alive through Jesus Christ. This is a phenomenal thought! This is talking about how you were spiritually dead until you became a Believer and now you are spiritually alive!

To be spiritually dead is to see yourself as someone who lives a life for themselves, consuming everything around them for their own pleasure and amusement. You realize that you are selfish and that this keeps you from having a relationship with God, who can't stand selfishness in people. You heard and received the story of Jesus Christ dying on the cross as payment for all of your sins. You heard about God raising Christ from the dead through the power of the Holy Spirit so that you, too, will be raised to live with God for eternity. You see, this is the thought: you were a dirty, rotten-to-the-core, low-down, good-for-nothing, spiritually dead sinner with no hope. Because of Jesus Christ, God has made you a new creation with eternity as your hope.

It is that thought that brings Believers to the point of "offering" themselves to God. With this thought constantly on our minds as Believers, we will find it easier to offer ourselves to God.

But don't forget that you have to offer yourself to God! The verse above says that there is another that you could offer yourself to, and this is what all Believers have done far too many times. As a Believer, you could offer yourself to sin as an instrument of unrighteousness (definitely not God). This "offer" is insidious because the "ME" in me has more interest in me than in others. This happens when Believers become so wrapped up with the things of this world that they are oblivious to offering themselves to sin.

This is when we have given in to sin, and we don't even realize it. We are distracted by how tired we are, or how frustrated we are with others, or how nothing ever seems to go the way we want it to go, or asking why do these things always happen to me, or anything that involves the "you" in you. When you give into "yourself," you are offering yourself to sin as an instrument of unrighteousness. Most of us would recoil at thinking this way about ourselves...but it is the spiritual truth that when left to ourselves, we will be thinking only of ourselves and not of others and certainly not of God.

The bottom line to all of this is a paradox: you realize how bad you are so that God can make you as righteous as Jesus. In other words, while

I believe that I am the lowest and worst of sinners, I believe that God sent His Son, Jesus Christ, to suffer all of the judgment that God has a right to hold me accountable for. I go from realizing just how bad I am to how GREAT God is! I am now a child of God because of His love, mercy, and grace. That thought is sufficient to keep my mind on God and others and not myself. How about you?

Are you continuously in love with God and other people? This is the greatest command that Jesus gave. He would not have said it if He thought you couldn't do it. Love God and serve others – it doesn't get any simpler.

3

YOUR LIFE
SHOULD BE LIGHT

For you were once darkness, but now you are light in the
Lord. Live as children of light (for the fruit of the light
consists in all goodness, righteousness and truth) and find
out what pleases the Lord.

—Ephesians 5:8-10

FOR A LONG TIME, I had been misreading these verses. I thought that I
was once "in" darkness and, as a Believer, I was now living "in" the
light. I think the reason I misread these verses for so long is that I could
not comprehend what it meant by being "darkness" and being "light."
This is a powerful and deep spiritual truth. Read the verses again. If
you are a Believer, you are light! This is not easy to accept. It is like
believing that you could not be considered light because most of us have
an ingrained opinion that we are sinners and we always have the potential
to disobey God.

Well, we are sinners and we will disobey God! That's great news, isn't
it? But, where do we spend most of our time thinking? What should we
be doing? Should we spend it on watching out for the next sin that we
commit? Should we always be evaluating whether something we are about
to do is in God's will or not? I don't think God intended us to waste our
time managing our sin problems. Instead, I think God is saying, "Look
what I have done for you through my Son, Jesus Christ! His death has paid

9

for all of your sins (past, present, and future) and His resurrection ensures that you will be resurrected and will live with Me for eternity!" Do you think maybe you would have a different view of what you are doing in your life if you could keep this thought in your head? I think so!

Being "light" means that as you live in this world you will have a glow about you. It won't be a physical glow that people can see. Instead, it will be what this verse says is "goodness, righteousness, and truth." This is the fruit of your thinking about what God has done for you instead of you managing your sins. Others will see your life as complete, peaceful, abundant, and something that they would like to have. When you think about God doing everything He can to have an intimate and personal relationship with you, your life will be light.

Another way to look at yourself as being light is to consider "light" from a weight perspective. No matter what you weigh, your life will be light. The burdens of this world will not be weighing you down to the point that you become depressed, anxious, sluggish, and worrisome. Your thoughts will be light. The decisions that you have to make will be considered light as you remember what God has done for you. Relationships with others will be from God's perspective and not your own.

As these verses say, when you live your life as "light," you will discover what pleases the Lord. I know when I first began to love my wife, I wanted to find out what pleased her and to do those things. This is how you should pursue living your life on this earth – finding what pleases God and then doing it. But, this discovery can be done only when you are light. The things of this earth will grow darker as you ponder the wondrous acts of God that have occurred throughout your life. When you base the next moment you live on God's unconditional love for you, you will be light and that light will shine in the darkest corners of this world. And, others will see that light!

Can you imagine being with a person who is light - a person who is all about "goodness, righteousness, and truth"? Wouldn't you like to be that person so that others will come to know who God is in your life? This is the way God intended for us to be His witness to others in this world. To be light where there is only darkness.

Spend time each day thinking of what God did for you yesterday. If you cannot think of one thing, you are blind, and deaf. Ask someone what they saw you do yesterday – you will start to find God in the smallest things.

4

YOUR LIFE
WHATEVER IT TAKES!

> Then the LORD said to Satan, "Have you considered
> my servant Job? There is no one on earth like him;
> He is blameless and upright, a man who fears God and
> shuns evil."
>
> —JOB 1:8

I WANT YOU TO KNOW that I have intentionally avoided using this verse in *Life- Changing Verses*. It is an extremely difficult verse to comprehend and accept as coming from a loving God. The setting for God saying this was a call by God for all angels to give Him a report. Satan was one of the angels that had to report. During this reporting, God initiated (and, that's what makes this a hard verse) a conversation about one of God's best servants on this earth, a man named Job. He (God) asked Satan if he (Satan) had ever noticed Job. Now, everything would be OK if this was just a discussion between God and Satan, but it's not.

What comes out of this conversation is an attack by Satan on Job. Most people know that Job lost everything he had (wealth, children and his own health) except his wife. Remember that this loss was because of Satan's attacks that were initiated, approved, and observed by God. WOW!! This will set anyone's heart to skip a beat or even stop beating. The book of Job is known as a book about suffering, because Job suffers. It is also about why bad things happen to good people. But, it is ultimately about the value that God places on having a right relationship with Him..."whatever it takes!"

We know that Job is a good man, because God says he is. The suffering is easy to understand because Job loses all he has. Would you want to be in Job's shoes and have God ask Satan, "Consider my servant <your name>"? I don't think anyone would want that! So, why would God hand Job over to Satan when Job was blameless, upright and feared God? Make sure you have the picture! The best person on earth from God's point of view is given over by God to the most evil angel to wreak havoc on his earthly life.

This did not sit well with me when I first read the book of Job. I wanted to run, duck, and hide from God, so that He wouldn't see me and ask Satan the same thing! This is like when someone in the church is looking for a volunteer...you don't want them to make eye contact with you for fear that you will be noticed. In the case of Job, he did not have the opportunity to run, duck, and hide. God singled him out. What in the Kingdom of God is going on? All during the book of Job, he and his three friends are trying to determine why all this bad stuff happened to Job. They think that Job must have sinned; therefore, God is getting back at him. This is bad theology because nothing in the book of Job tells us that God was punishing Job for some sin. But, just like Job, we want to ask God and have Him tell us why bad things happen to good people. What possible purpose could God have to allow a person to suffer so greatly? I think all of us can identify with Job's suffering.

When you get toward the end of Job you find out what God's purpose was for Job's life. Job had a very strong relationship with God. But, Job's relationship with God was based on Job's understanding of God. God saw in Job's heart that there was something not right in his acceptance of God. Now, this is important...God also knew that the ONLY WAY Job would understand what was wrong was through intense suffering. God had to get Job to a point of desperation where Job had to cry out to God, "WHY?" When Job did that, God told him.

You see, Job had become so comfortable with himself in his relationship with God that he (Job) began to take God for granted. When the suffering came on Job, he "demanded" an answer from God. Job thought he had a right to get an answer from God. Job thought of himself so highly that God had to explain why he was suffering. Do you see Job's arrogance? God saw this in Job before God said to Satan, "Consider my servant Job."

God has a purpose for everything, and He does not owe us an

explanation for anything. God is Sovereign. That means He can do whatever He wants, whenever He wants, in any way He wants, without owing us a reason. Instead of demanding that God owes us, we should be saying to Him, "God, whatever it takes for me to be all that you want, then do it." We should be looking at all the bad stuff that happens to us as a way that God is teaching and cleansing us from our own worldly way of living. This is extremely difficult, but doable – just ask Job!

5

JESUS CHRIST
HOW DO YOU SEE HIM?

> He could not do any miracles there, except lay his hands
> on a few sick people and heal them. And he was amazed
> at their lack of faith.
>
> —MARK 6:5-6

THIS IS AN AMAZING DESCRIPTION of the work of Jesus Christ while ministering to people on earth. Actually, it's kind of sad when Jesus wanted to help others but because of their lack of faith, He was limited in His work. Now, I know that you are probably thinking that Jesus Christ could do whatever He wished to do, because He is God and has the power of the Holy Spirit to do unbelievable miracles. So, how and why does our lack of faith limit God's work?

May I suggest that you read the complete context of these verses (Mark 6:1-6). What happens is that Jesus goes back to the town where He was raised as a child. The people there knew Jesus, but only as the "carpenter's son" and not the Son of God. They realized that Jesus had done miracles, but they knew where He lived as a child. They knew His parents and His brothers and sisters. This knowledge limited their thinking about Jesus being the Son of God. They could think of Jesus only as a child running around and playing with other children.

I think that this may be a similar problem for a lot of Believers. We develop a picture in our mind of who Jesus is, and we carry it around with us for the rest of our lives. The problem with that (as it was with the Nazarenes in the home town of Jesus) is we cannot continue to learn about who Jesus is because of our preconceived thoughts. Our understanding of Jesus is limited.

For example, many Believers see Jesus as a baby in a manger. Some artists have painted pictures of a man with a beard who appears gentle, caring, and in a thoughtful pose. Every time you hear the name "Jesus," that picture may pop into your head. Some Believers can picture Jesus only dying on the cross. Others picture an empty tomb and a brightly clothed Jesus. Whatever picture pops into your head when you hear the name "Jesus" has been developed throughout your lifetime. The potential problem with this is that we limit our understanding of Jesus Christ. When put together, many Believers have the understanding that Jesus began in a manger, spent about 33 years on earth, died on the cross, and was resurrected after three days. It is difficult for many Believers to think of Jesus outside of His life on this earth. And, that holds us back in exercising our faith...just like the Nazarenes.

Can you see that Believers who are settled in their understanding of Jesus will grow to a point of not believing that God can work a miracle in their lives? Because of our lack of faith, we limit God to only those things that are congruent with our understanding of Jesus Christ. When our knowledge of Jesus becomes stagnant and limited, we cannot see God at work. I think that this is the limitation in worldly people seeing the real power of God at work.

Consider only the following about Him. Jesus Christ is God! He was with God at the beginning of everything even before anything was created. Everything was created by Jesus and is sustained today by Him. He appeared in bodily form several times in the Old Testament. In the future, He will defeat all of the earth's armies and Satan and all of his demons. He will judge Believers on the works they perform as Christians on this earth. He will finish God's plan for redeeming this world and all of His children.

So, how should we think on Jesus Christ? His time from the manger to the tomb is nothing compared to His existing with God before there was anything and after everything comes to an end by Him. His activities throughout the history of Creation continue to give maturing Believers a view of God's love, grace, and forgiveness. Do you have a limited view of Jesus Christ like the Nazarenes or do you allow the Holy Spirit to show you things that makes miracles and eternity more real than the world you are living in? Get to know more about Jesus by reading the New Testament and highlighting references to Jesus. The four gospels and the book of Hebrews would be a great start.

6

GOD

WILL JUDGE THROUGH CHRIST

> This will take place on the day when God will judge men's
> secrets through Jesus Christ, as my gospel declares.
>
> —ROMANS 2:16

IT TOOK ME A LONG time as a Believer to understand that Jesus Christ will judge. I guess I always had Christ pictured in my mind as Savior and not as a judge. But this verse says that when God judges, He will do it through Jesus Christ. That seems pretty clear to me yet very hard to comprehend.

I believe that the context of the verse above is saying that everyone will be judged by the revelation God has given them. For example, the Old Testament saints did not have the cross or the blood of Christ to forgive their sins. Some of them had only the blood of lambs, goats, and bulls. And others did not have even that. Yet, God will hold each one of them responsible for what He has shown them. This is true for the Israelites who saw many manifestations of God and for the Gentiles who God revealed Himself to through many ways in their lives. God will hold them accountable for what He has shown them. And, I know this is a stretch, but I believe that every single man, woman, and child has seen the essence of Jesus Christ (see John 8:56-59) and God has given them ample opportunity to accept or reject those revelations. Therefore, no one will stand before God with an excuse for not accepting His revelation to them.

The verse above also describes another element of God's judgment when it refers to "men's secrets." With that wording, I know that no man or woman will have any excuse that God will accept. This applies to the person who "behaves like a Believer" but is not depending on Jesus Christ for forgiveness of sins. In other words, when all of us (me, you, your best friend, etc.) stand in judgment before God, we will not be able to fool God like we did everyone here on earth. No Christian pretenders can get by God's judgment. The reason is stated in this verse. God will judge everyone's secret life within themselves. God will see what is truly in their hearts when they have worshipped Him. God also will know what motivated them when they served others. If you're wondering if you will get away with some selfish motives in serving others or ritualistic worship of God, I can tell you, you don't stand a chance! God knows your secrets and He will judge them through Jesus Christ.

Why Jesus Christ? Because Jesus is our Savior – He suffered the judgment of our sins that God intended for us (i.e., separation from God). Because Jesus is our Lord – He was raised from the dead by the power of the Holy Spirit so that the life we live on this earth would be empowered by the Holy Spirit. As a new creation, God has given us everything to live a holy life on this earth through the Holy Spirit. Therefore, Believers are asked by Jesus Christ to "Deny yourself, pick up your cross daily and follow Me." (See Luke 9:23.)

Finally, although our sins have been judged and Jesus Christ has forgiven us of those sins, He still looks at how each of us lived our life as a Believer. The "work" we do as a Believer will be judged by Christ. Anything and everything that was done with selfish motives or ambitions will be considered as of no value. For example, if you gave a million dollars to a church or a charity with the appearance of self sacrifice when, in actuality, you were looking for a tax write-off or personal fame, then that act of giving would be worth nothing when judged by Christ.

Jesus is looking for genuine Believers (disciples) who will live a selfless life totally dedicated to the worship of God and the serving of others. When God judges your secrets there will be nothing for you to be ashamed of or want to hide from Him. Know that your judgment for entrance into heaven was assumed by Christ. Your works after becoming a Christian will determine your rewards in heaven, not your salvation.

7

YOUR LIFE
FILLED WITH INEXPRESSIBLE JOY

> Though you have not seen him, you love him; and even
> though you do not see him now, you believe in him and
> are filled with an inexpressible and glorious joy.
>
> —1 PETER 1:8

THE NEXT TIME YOU GET around a bunch of Believers, observe closely
how they look. Are they depressed? Do they look like they have been
sucking on some lemons? Are they suspicious looking? Do they look like
their team just lost the biggest game of the year? Are they stone faced –
unsmiling? Do they look or act like the world owes them something? You
get the picture. These "appearances" reflect the attitude of those people
you are seeing. What about you?

Do you put on different faces depending on who you are with? For
example, for a spouse, you put on a face that says that you have been out in
the world facing all kinds of problems and you deserve to look tired, worn
out, and in need of a trip to the spa. Many times during a typical, average
day, we will wear certain "attitudes" to get something we want. We even
think to ourselves, "No harm done." But what are you saying about your
life as it is lived for Christ? That's the rub.

You see in the verse above how a real Believer should appear: "filled
with inexpressible and glorious joy." WOW!! There are so many Christians
that are so far away from glorious joy that you begin to think that what

others say about Christians is true. "If you are a Christian, then you can't have fun...you must look serious about everything, because God is serious." Matter of fact, I'd go so far as to say that some Christians who see another Christian with "inexpressible joy" will do and say anything to bring that joyful brother or sister back down to what they call "reality." Give me a break! But it's true! If a "serious" Christian sees an "inexpressibly joyful" Christian, the serious Christian will use all kinds of logic and rationale to say that there is something "wrong" with that joyful Christian. "Someone please throw a bucket of cold water on that joyful Christian!" "He/she is not living in the real world." Well, I say, PRAISE THE LORD!! I'd rather be living a joyful life in the Kingdom of God than a depressing life in this world. How about you?

A Believer who loves God and believes that Christ died for their sins has an attitude of inexpressible joy. They can't help it! They see everything from an eternal perspective and that perspective is living forever in the presence of the Lord God Almighty. WOW!!

A Believer who spends most of their time focusing on the things of this world will reflect the attitude of this world. What are the attitudes of this world? 1) You have to take care of yourself because no one else cares. 2) You have to get all you can while you can because you may not be able to get it later. 3) You are always right and everyone else is wrong. 4) You deserve to be happy...God wants you happy, so you should only be involved with things that make you happy.

These four statements reflect the attitudes of cynicism, materialism, egotism, and selfishness respectively. But, what's so sad is that these are the acceptable attitudes of this world; and, what is sadder is that these are attitudes of a lot of Christians. An attitude of glorious joy will be ridiculed, attacked, and disregarded because, now listen to this, it is not of this world. Is this not the truth about our living our lives on this earth? We are only strangers passing though this world. Nothing of this world should stick to us.

This verse should be a measuring stick for the attitude of your life as a Believer. I know some of you are going to justify some worry, depression, and all of the other "anti–inexpressible joy" attitudes because you just can't believe that such a thing can exist in this world. Guess what? If you think that way, then you have bought into the philosophy of this world that says there is no such thing as "glorious joy" because this world is so bad. Well, think on the world and you'll get depressed. Think on God and Christ and you will have inexpressible and glorious joy...and your attitude will be unworldly. I say again, PRAISE THE LORD!

One last thing is when we, as Believers, slip into an attitude of apathy or bitterness as we reflect on our own circumstances. This will happen to all of us at some time during our lives. But the Bible says to encourage one another. Use the spiritual gift that God has given you to build up others. Always remind others of what God has done for them through Christ. Remind them of His unconditional love. Point them toward the future reality of the second coming of Christ and an eternal life lived with Him.

Now, that will produce inexpressible and glorious joy in the middle of this cynical, materialistic, egotistical, and self-centered world. Do this for other Believers and you will find your own attitude changed, even though you didn't do anything to change it yourself. All of the commands are summed up as follows: "Love God and serve others." In this is inexpressible and glorious joy.

8

GOD

HAS PREPARED YOU FOR

DIVINE ENCOUNTERS

For if you remain silent at this time, relief and deliverance
for the Jews will arise from another place, but you and
your father's family will perish. And who knows but that
you have come to royal position for such a time as this?

—ESTHER 4:14

THIS VERSE DESCRIBES THE LIFE-THREATENING position that a woman
found herself in while part of a very high level of government. The
lives of all the Jews that were living in a certain country were at stake.
This was to be the first "holocaust" of the Jews. All the Jews were to be
destroyed by a command from the king of that country. The person was
Queen Esther, a Jew married to the King. She was being asked by her uncle
to intercede on behalf of all Jews at the risk of her own life before the king.
When you read this verse, her uncle tells her that if she doesn't act, then
relief and deliverance will come from someone else. This is a reference to
God's protection of the Jews. If Esther did not intercede, then God would
find another person.

You see, God knew before Esther was born that there would be a
time for her to "speak up" for God (a divine encounter). God knew that
some people would try to destroy all of the Jews. Therefore, God put into

motion His will for the King of Persia to select Esther from numerous other women to make her queen. God had provided her uncle to encourage her during this time. Now, what would happen if Esther disobeyed God (i.e., not do His will)? God would have had someone else ready to speak up because of His covenant with Israel.

Her uncle told her that God had prepared her for just this incident (a divine encounter). When you think of all of the events leading up to Esther being queen and being in a position to save all of the Jews, there is no way you could call this "fortunate" or "lucky" or "chance." As Believers, we need to know that there's no such thing as "coincidence" in our lives. It was God's will! Nothing in this world can stop or alter God's will for eternity. His "will" will be done. His plans for eternity will be carried out and come to full completion. He prepares divine encounters so that we can tell others about Him. However, as Believers, we can disobey God by refusing to allow His will into our lives. Just like Esther, God will carry out His will even if we don't. This can be both comforting and scary.

Comforting - if we know that others are doing God's will. We know that God is working through other Believers to share the gospel with those who live outside our country, or those who live in the inner cities of our country, or even those who live in our neighborhood. Some of us can be safely on the sidelines cheering others on. This is comforting to us because someone else is taking the risk.

Scary - if we are one of those who are to fulfill God's will. It's what we pray when we say the Lord's Prayer: "Your will be done on earth as it is in heaven." It's just that many of us want to add, "As long as your will is done by others." But I think God has prepared each one of us for divine encounters. No Believer is relieved of this expectation from God. God gives every one of us divine encounters and we should be obedient to His divine will.

God's will involves His plan that He worked out before He created the heavens and the earth: to make right the relationship (that man destroyed through sin) between God and man. He uses Believers to reveal His plan to others. He uses precise things at exactly the right moment to reveal Himself to those who do not know Him: a divine encounter. These divine encounters are opportunities to demonstrate our strong faith and trust in Him so that others will come to know Him.

Therefore, as Believers we are all placed in similar positions as Queen Esther. We are asked to share our life in Christ with others no matter the cost. When we do this, God's eternal will is being done. Through divine encounters, He asks you to obey Him and to tell others about the love, forgiveness, and grace that God has given you. Tell them what He has done to give you an abundant life in a world gone crazy. God has prepared you for divine encounters. Don't miss any of them!

9

LOVE

THE WORLD OR THE LOVE OF GOD? – PART 1

> Do not love the world or anything in the world. If anyone loves the world, the love of the Father is not in him. For everything in the world—the cravings of sinful man, the lust of his eyes and the boasting of what he has and does—comes not from the Father but from the world. The world and its desires pass away, but the man who does the will of God lives forever.
>
> —1 JOHN 2:15-17

THESE VERSES ARE PRETTY CLEAR on loving the world versus having the love of God in our lives. Note that it is our "loving" the world as compared to our "having" the love of God. It is sort of like the love of the world comes from within us toward the things in this world while the love of God is something that comes to us. As Believers, the love of the Father is in us until we love the things of the world. Then, the love of the Father is not in us. Wouldn't it be nice if God made His love a permanent part of our lives so that we would not love the world? It won't happen! God created free will within us so that we would willingly choose Him and not the world. Therefore, as Believers, we need to be aware of the fact that when we grow to love something in this world, we will be making the love of God null and void in our lives.

Our love for this world is to use, abuse, and consume things for ourselves. The only decision regarding this kind of love would be for you to ask, "What will make me happy?" We are driven to love the things of this world when we place our condition for happiness on those things. Some of these things are literally "things" – houses, cars, boats, HDTVs, etc. Even jobs, careers, and hobbies can become things that we place ahead of our relationships with others (spouse and children). But, even our spouse or our children can become "things" of this world when we choose them for our happiness, and they become more important than the love of the Father. We can actually love our spouse and children deeper with God's love than the love of the world.

An example of love for this world is my early love for football. To watch football games on TV or to listen to Larry Munson broadcast for the Georgia Bulldogs took priority over everything in my life (including my wife and kids). At the time, I did not realize that those "things" of the world were controlling me. But they were. I thought that my happiness was based on watching football games. Now, I regret missing the first six years of my son's life, and the first three years of my daughter's life, and, most importantly, the seven years I missed with my wife because I loved watching football games. And, you know what? I don't remember any of those games. As a matter of fact, my emotions dominated my life as to whether my teams won or loss. In other words, the things of this world affected the way I related to my family and others.

The things of this world are made to take you captive, to give you a false sense of happiness, and to negatively impact every relationship you have. Let me repeat that: the things of this world are made to deceive you regarding what will make you happy. I think you can enjoy the things of this world but don't expect that they will bring you happiness. That's where we go terribly wrong.

We all are in love with the things of this world - at least in our materialistic, consumer-oriented society. That's what materialism and consumerism is all about…getting you to buy something to make you happy when it won't. That's what these verses are saying to us. All of us should admit it and move on.

We live in the United States of America where life is good. When I say "good," I mean as compared to other places in this world where finding something to eat is to survive for one more day. At the same time, there are people who have forsaken the comforts of living in America to live in other places not so pleasant just to demonstrate the love of God to others.

There are a few who have given up much to work and live in inner cities and other tough places even in the U.S. But, most Believers are very content to stay where they are. Why? Because, quite frankly, we love the things of this world. If Believers practiced these verses where they lived (even in the U.S. or, even in their own city), there would be many who would turn to God because they would see Believers who have the love of God in their lives.

God has a love that He wants to give to each of us. It is interesting that the most famous verse from the Bible is "For **God so loved the world** that He gave His one and only Son, that whoever believes in him shall not perish but have eternal life." You know this as John 3:16. His love is a decision to love us unconditionally. You see the love of the Father has an object in mind and that object is us – you, me, and every single human being. His love for the world was for us. He literally sacrificed Himself for you. And, He wants you to love others with His love.

Our love for the things of this world is not for others – it is for ourselves and that creates all kinds of relationship problems. In the next chapter, we will consider the "cravings," "lust," and "boasting" that result in damaged relationships and an unfulfilled life. In the meantime, consider what you love in this world for yourself as opposed to the love of the Father that has been given to you to love others.

10

LOVE

THE WORLD OR THE LOVE OF GOD? – PART 2

Do not love the world or anything in the world. If anyone loves the world, the love of the Father is not in him. For everything in the world—the cravings of sinful man, the lust of his eyes and the boasting of what he has and does—comes not from the Father but from the world. The world and its desires pass away, but the man who does the will of God lives forever.

—1 JOHN 2:15-17

IN THE LAST CHAPTER I discussed the two kinds of love in these verses: one kind that comes from within us, and the other kind is the love of the Father that comes from Him. In this chapter I want to look at what there is to love in this world and why it is so damaging to relationships. Reread the verses above.

The "cravings of sinful man" will literally make you a slave to things of this world – you will become just like a drug addict and have to have another "fix." These cravings will make you do things that under normal conditions you would not do – you will act irrationally without realizing that it is irrational. You'll spend time and money on things that, in the long run, are unimportant. But, at the time of the craving, you are convinced that this is the only thing that will make you happy.

A sure sign of the "cravings of sinful man" is when your personality changes, because somebody (including your own family) stands between you and your cravings. You say, "Nobody had better mess with me! I've got a craving to satisfy!" This is just plain ugly to see (and that's how I see myself when I was so involved with football – just plain ugly!).

The "lust of your eyes" will distract you from the beauty that God has put into this world. The word "lust" is much like the word "cravings." You will slowly become addicted to watching things that are not beneficial for your spiritual growth. These things take the form of everything seen in this world: newspapers, magazines, movies, TV, books, and the internet. One of the most damaging aspects of the "lust of his eyes" occurs when a man gives in to pornography.

Let me be very clear: every lust after anything pornographic DAMAGES that man's relationship with others – especially, his wife. As one person put it, "Fifty percent of Christians say pornography is a problem in their home, and the other half are in denial." Be honest with yourself about the lust in you, because it is in all of us.

The "boasting of what you have done and do" is a relationship killer. Too many times I've heard how a person avoids someone else because all they talk about is themselves. I think the root problem with boasting about one's self is not being aware of who you are in Christ. As a Believer, everything about our past is over with and done. A Believer who feels that they must rehash the past to obtain the respect of others is totally deceived by this world. They have accepted the philosophy of this world that says you must take care of yourself because no one else will.

As Believers, we rest on the promises of God who loves us and cares for us rather than the moments in the past that seemed to satisfy our egos. Those moments are GONE! Leave them in the past! All they do is prop up your ego to feel superior to others. That is not the life of a Believer.

The bottom line to these verses is that we are all guilty of loving things in this world. God knows that. Yet, He continues to transform our lives from being totally consumed by the "self" in us to one that is directed toward Him and others. The abundant life that Christ has given us is available as we quit loving the things in this world and accept the love of the Father. Consider your decisions from eternity's point of view and not from the momentary worldly pleasure that damages relationships with others. You have this decision to make every day of your life.

11

GOD

DO YOU READ OR STUDY HIS WORD?

For the gracious hand of his God was on him. For Ezra had devoted himself to the study and observance of the Law of the LORD, and to teaching its decrees and laws in Israel.

—EZRA 7:9B-10

I DON'T KNOW ABOUT YOU but I love the verses above. I am in awe when I think of all of the intelligence that people have put into the study of the Bible (God's Word). No other book has been studied and read as much as the Bible. It's like comparing the distance from the earth to the moon (the Bible), to the distance from your home to your mailbox (any other book).

No other book is like it. And yet, many Believers try to live a Christian life without reading the Bible and by relying on others to explain it. Some Believers try to understand the Bible using only their own mental capabilities. Most Believers desire to read the Bible but find it too difficult and hard to understand. If this is you, please read on.

From my own experience, I was woefully uninformed about the Bible until I was 30 years old. Before I was 30, I had taught Bible study classes (children's classes and a few discipleship classes). But I wasn't teaching the

Bible with a dependence on the Holy Spirit to reveal His Word to me. I tried to understand the Bible through my own intellect. I failed miserably and I felt miserable! I asked God, "Why do you make your Word so hard to understand?"

I was 30 years old when God finally got through to me that understanding His Word had nothing to do with my intellectual capacity (or lack thereof) or what others would tell me about the Bible. It all had to do with knowing that it is God's Word and that He would reveal to me truths about His Word through the Holy Spirit. There was no way for me to understand it no matter how hard I tried. I discovered that my motive in reading and studying His Word was for the self in me. That is, I wanted to understand it to become a better Christian and to appear to others that I understood the Bible. What rotten, selfish motives I had!

When I was 30, I saw the need to devote myself to God and His Word as opposed to trying to understand it, so that I or others would think that I knew the Bible. The most significant change occurred when I saw God's story of redemption and how He wanted to reveal that story throughout the Bible. In other words, I sensed within myself a deep and sincere need to know God and what He wanted to reveal to me.

My focus went from trying to know His Word to wanting to know Him through His Word. My Bible reading and studying totally changed. For the next 35 years, my desire to know Him through His Word has never let up. Many times I thought it would dry up and go away, but it hasn't. The more I read and study His Word about Him, the more I want to know about Him.

I believe that God has given you the revelation of His Word that is needed for you to live a Christian life in today's world. But, you have to read and study His Word from His perspective. As Ezra devoted himself to the study of God's Word, so should all Believers. Read and study His Word to know God and to know Him better than anyone else on this earth. His Word is not confusing or difficult when we begin to see His work from creating us to redeeming us to preparing us to live with Him for eternity. That's what the Bible is all about – Him!

12

FAITH

HOW MUCH DO YOU HAVE?

When Jesus heard this, he was amazed at him, and turning
to the crowd following him, he said, "I tell you, I have
not found such great faith even in Israel."

—LUKE 7:9

THIS IS AN AMAZING STATEMENT coming from Jesus while He was
ministering on this earth. The background of this verse is that a
Roman Centurion (a man with significant power and authority) knew
that one of his most valued servants was sick and dying. The Centurion
had heard about this man named "Jesus" and about His healing power.
The Centurion wanted Jesus to come to his house to heal the servant.
But, instead of going himself, the Centurion asked some older Jews to go
to Jesus and ask him to come and heal his servant. Jesus heard the pleas of
these Jews and went to the Centurion's house.

Before Jesus came near the house, the Centurion sent some of his
friends to Jesus to tell him not to enter his house. The reason for this was
that the Centurion did not feel worthy for Jesus to be in his house. He did
not even feel worthy enough to talk with Jesus. Instead, the Centurion
equated his authority with that of Jesus. If the Centurion gave an order,
it was to be obeyed. He reasoned that if Jesus gave an order, it would be
obeyed, even when it came to healing a sick person.

Throughout this story you should remember that pious religious Jews were forbidden to enter the house of a Gentile. If they did, they would be considered unclean. At the same time, the Roman soldiers considered the Jews not worthy of any consideration (Jews were under the bondage of Roman rule). Yet, here is a Centurion who appeared to have all of this upside down. He, as a Gentile, was not worthy to associate with Jesus. And, Jesus, as a Jew, was not to associate with a Gentile. But the Centurion did not allow these conditions to restrict his faith in Jesus.

Also, note that Jesus compared the faith of the Centurion with that of His own people, Israel. This is like saying that Jesus could find people outside of your church that have more faith than those of you who belong to a church. WOW!! That hits home!

There is another verse in the Bible that says, "Without faith it is impossible to please God." (See Hebrews 11:6.) Do you think that God uses the amount of faith that we demonstrate in tough times to set us apart from the world? I believe so. He did that with setting the Centurion apart from all of Israel. How often do you actually put your faith in God? When times are rough and tough, do you trust the words of God when He says, "I will never leave you or forsake you"? How much faith do you have in the promise of God? The amount is demonstrated by how tough your situation is.

Jesus was amazed at the Centurion's faith. Do you think that you could amaze Him with your faith? Unfortunately, many of us, as Believers, are just like the disciples of Jesus. They spent three years with Jesus and all Jesus could say to them was, "You of little faith." I don't think it's how much time you spend reading the Bible or going to church or giving tithes and offerings that demonstrates the amount of faith you have in God.

The amount of faith you have in God is demonstrated at those times in your life when He asks you to give yourself totally to do something for Him. And this always involves a sacrifice which requires faith. This can occur with your Bible reading, going to church, and giving; but, I think you can see from the example of the Centurion that "amazement" occurs when there are no conditions on what you do for Him.

Most of us add conditions on what we think God wants us to do. This limits God's work in our lives. In other words, by your lack of faith, you limit the miraculous work of God in your life. Allow God to work through your life today, not expecting that God will make it easier and more comfortable, but to use you so that others may come to know who He is. This requires great faith and is sorely needed in the world today.

13

GOD

SECRET THINGS AND
REVEALED THINGS

> The secret things belong to the LORD our God, but the
> things revealed belong to us and to our children forever,
> that we may follow all the words of this law.
>
> —DEUTERONOMY 29:29

THIS IS AN UNUSUAL VERSE to find in the Bible. Through Moses, God's
Holy Spirit is letting us know that there are things that God will
not tell us. At the same time, there are things that God reveals to us
and our children so that we will have a strong and healthy relationship
with Him.

This verse appears near the end of the first five books of the Old
Testament (called the "Torah"). These five books (Genesis – Deuteronomy)
tell us so much about Creation and how God was forming Israel (Hebrews)
into a nation. The Hebrews had been through a lot. God had set them free
from slavery in Egypt. God told them many things about who He is and
how He wanted them to be His people.

One of the most amazing aspects of God's revelation to the Hebrews
was that He was not like any of the idols that they saw in Egypt. He
manifested Himself through powerful images of the ten plagues in Egypt,
a "pillar of fire," invisible forces separating a sea, and many others. But He

was not a stone or wood figure made by man. This verse is toward the end of all of these revelations from God to the Hebrews. Read it again with this background in mind.

How does this apply to us today? Well, in my opinion, modern man has developed a principle of living that says, "There is nothing that I cannot know...I can know anything and everything." In some cases, we have become so arrogant that we even say, "I know everything!" With that kind of attitude, can you see there is no need for God? This is the driving force behind all of the man-created theories of evolution, existence of man, life on other planets, etc. So, God says in this verse that He will not tell us everything.

Why does God withhold things from us? I can think of two reasons. The first is this attitude of knowing everything and not needing God. Man has yet to figure out how to live with each other. No government, no community, no cult, and no anything of man has been successful in living together over time.

Every world empire has failed. Every government structure has failed. Every philosophy of man has failed. To bring it down to me and you, we just don't know how to run our own lives successfully. Therefore, God says, "I will tell you only those things that will give you the true meaning of life and, in particular, your life." You don't have to know everything to live a joyful and peaceful life.

The second reason God withholds things from us is that we are puny-brained, finite, short-lived creatures that cannot handle all of the mysteries of life, the universe, and those things that have yet to be seen (heaven). For this reason, God says that all Believers will receive a new body that is eternal as opposed to our existing bodies that grow old and die. When that happens to you, you will begin to understand all of the things that God has not revealed to you, and you will stand in holy awe of who He is. At that time, you will know Him as He is. Right now, you can't take all of Him and He knows it.

In the meantime, God says clearly that He will reveal to you those things necessary for you to live a life for Him on this earth. He may or may not include "worldly wisdom" so that you can become wealthy or smart or famous on this earth. But He will definitely reveal to you things that will give you "spiritual wisdom."

Some of the things that God reveals are: His unconditional love, His free grace, His longing to have a personal relationship with you, and many others. For example, as you begin to understand His forgiveness (revealed through Jesus Christ), you can begin to forgive others – really forgive them! As you understand His eternal purpose for your life and that He loves you just the way you are, you will be set free from the fleshly drive to be accepted in this world.

God looks at wisdom of knowing things in this order:

1. Know the secret things of God (when you live with Him for eternity)

2. Know the revelations that God has given you (to live a Godly life on this earth)

3. Know how to get ahead in this world (to get worldly things so that you can look good to others)

Unfortunately, most of us put number 3 as our number 1 and give no time to number 2. If you want to live the life that God has given you to its fullest and in the most abundant way, then consider how He has revealed Himself to you through His Word and through your own life (number 2 above). God has worked in everyone's life; it's just that we don't take the time to see His work in our lives. In Colossians 3, God's Word says to seek those things which are above and not the things on this earth. What do you spend most of your time seeking? Number 2 or number 3?

14

YOUR LIFE
STAYING ON COURSE

But now that you know God—or rather are known by God—how is it that you are turning back to those weak and miserable principles? Do you wish to be enslaved by them all over again?

—GALATIANS 4:9

WHEN YOU ACCEPTED JESUS CHRIST as your Lord and Savior, numerous spiritual things happened:

Forgiveness: You received forgiveness of all of your past, present, and future sins. Jesus suffered and died on the cross with the punishment from God for your sins. God not only forgives all of your sins, but He forgets them.

Eternal Life: You also received eternal life, meaning that you will come to know God and live with God forever.

Inheritance: Along with that came an inheritance from God, since you are now a child of God.

Citizenship: You received citizenship in heaven, allowing you to be in the presence of God.

Holy Spirit: You received the Holy Spirit as a guarantee for all of God's promises. Jesus said that He must leave this world so that the Holy Spirit will come and take up residence in every Believer forever. The Holy Spirit is given to you to lead you and guide you into TRUTH. He is to convict you of sin and righteousness. He provides the spiritual power for you to say and do miraculous things. The Holy Spirit comforts you and counsels you. You have been given the Holy Spirit to dwell within you.

New Creation: You have also become a new creation. The Bible says that everything in the past is gone and that every day in your life is brand new. God works in your life every moment of your life. He never stops! Even at your worst, God continues to work on you as one of His children. He never leaves you or forsakes you.

These are a few of the things that happened when you believed and accepted that Christ died for your sins.

The verse above is directed toward those Believers who have forgotten all of these things that God has given them. And, this is all of us...every Believer goes through times where our focus leaves God and goes to the things of this world. We actually begin to live as we did before Christ. People see us like they do everyone else in this world.

It is interesting that this verse opens with your knowing God but quickly redirects your thinking to something much more powerful – that you are known by God. I think it is a tremendously comforting thought that God knows you as a Believer. And, He knows you better than anyone and only wants the best for you. He never forgets you. He never stops thinking of you. He is always looking out for the next moment in your life.

The heart of the verse above is not the awareness of being known by God, but that even being known by God, you live your life as if none of what you know about God has any impact on your life. The "weak and miserable principles" are those things that you learned in the world that you thought would make you feel safe and comfortable. The problem is that everything in this world (and I mean everything) is temporary. You have to keep searching and struggling to reach what you think is a safe and comfortable position. God offers eternal security; the world offers temporary security at the cost of your life.

One day, I had a man ask me to give him the top ten things that God expected of him. His motivation for this list was that he could do those things if that's what God wanted. He expected that by doing those things God would give him a happy, safe, and comfortable life. It's not important if this man could do those ten things the rest of his life (not him or anyone can). The significance of his list was to keep control of his own life. Also, he didn't have to mess around with all this "relationship" stuff with God and others. His "life" would consist of a constant evaluation as to whether he was doing those ten things. Just think what would happen if he ever missed one! There goes his whole life down the drain.

All of us are just like that man. We want what we think is the best (and easiest) way for us to live life to its fullest. The verse above says it is not in this world. Rather, it is in an active, vibrant, strong, constant, living relationship with God. We get to know God through the revelation of Jesus Christ. The Holy Spirit reveals these spiritual things to us. This is the abundant life. Are you living the abundant life or are you back in bondage to the "principles" of this world? Decide today that you will focus on what God has done for you as opposed to what the world is doing to you.

15

JESUS
BOLDNESS FROM KNOWING HIM

When they saw the courage of Peter and John and realized
that they were unschooled, ordinary men, they were
astonished and they took note that these men had been
with Jesus.

—ACTS 4:13

THIS IS A VERY EXCITING verse for all Believers. Our courage to be a
Christian today is directly related to the amount of time we spend
getting to know Jesus. The more time we spend learning about Jesus, the
bolder and more confident we are to live a life that honors God. So, ask
yourself about your desire to learn all you can about Jesus.

I clearly remember times in my younger days, when I was more
interested in things other than Jesus Christ. In those early days I thought
"to know Christ" was to think about him being born, dying on a cross, and
being raised from the dead, which is the heart of the gospel. However, the
Bible says that our lives should be conformed to the image of Christ. This
doesn't mean that we die on a cross. It means that our life is similar to that
of Jesus while on this earth. It means that we treat others as Christ did. It
means that we take the bumps and bruises of this life as Christ did.

It means that we live our life by the guidance of the Holy Spirit as
Christ did. It means that we focus on God the Father as Christ did. It took
me a long time to understand that I needed to know more about Jesus

Christ in addition to His birth, death, and resurrection. Something tells me that most Christians need to understand this also.

Christ was focused on people in need: people who did not have a lot, who were hurting, the orphans and widows, the lame and blind, the ones who were not accepted by society. We spend a lot of time focused on movie stars, politicians, athletes, and others who are in the "news." We do crazy stuff just to get an autograph. While we are wasting our time on these kinds of people, we miss those who are hurting although they are standing right in front of us.

Christ suffered for being the Son of God. Religious leaders called him names and even called Jesus the son of Satan! We, as Believers, should not be bothered by those who want to make fun of our belief. We should not be ashamed to be called Christians. Christ also suffered for the judgment of our sins. However, we cannot and will not (Praise the Lord!) suffer as He suffered for our sins. His suffering for our sins is God's way of granting us citizenship in heaven.

Christ repeatedly said that He was led by the Spirit. The Holy Spirit led Jesus into the desert to be tempted by Satan. After this event Jesus returned to Galilee in the power of the Spirit. The Spirit raised Jesus from the dead. In the same way, a Believer should be led by the Holy Spirit. The Bible says that we are to walk in the Spirit. This means that we trust everything (including our life) to God and allow His Spirit to guide us through life and to empower us to do God's will.

Jesus Christ ALWAYS focused on what God wanted Him to do on earth. Jesus said that He did only what the Father did. Jesus said that what you see Him do is what the Father does. In other words, God revealed Himself to man through the life of Jesus Christ. If you want to get to know who God is and what He is about, then study the life of Christ on this earth. What you'll find is the spiritual understanding of God's love, God's forgiveness, God's grace, God's power, God's sovereignty, and more.

For example, during the Christmas Holidays, I wonder if many of us are more focused on all of the "stuff" that has to be done to try to have a nice Christmas rather than the true meaning of celebrating Christmas. You know that we, as Believers, are just as guilty as some of the retail stores in taking Christ out of Christmas. When we become totally focused on the "stuff" of Christmas, we, unknowingly, have taken Christ out of Christmas just like they have.

May I suggest that all of us, as Believers, begin to think about God becoming like us in a manger 2,000 years ago; that He grew up into a man; that He ministered to people and their needs; and, that He wanted everyone to know who His Heavenly Father was. Does your life have the same aspects of life that Jesus had? Make it a point to learn more about Jesus Christ...you will also learn a lot about God and yourself.

16

YOUR LIFE
A WAKE-UP CALL IN
SERVING OTHERS

An argument started among the disciples as to which of them would be the greatest. Jesus, knowing their thoughts, took a little child and had him stand beside him. Then he said to them, "Whoever welcomes this little child in my name welcomes me; and whoever welcomes me welcomes the one who sent me. For he who is least among you all—he is the greatest."

—LUKE 9:46-48

IN THE VERSES ABOVE, THE disciples of Jesus had become busy to the point that they were comparing notes on who had done the most and who would be the greatest in the Kingdom of God. Jesus needed to give them a "wake-up call."

Jesus needed to remind His disciples about what the Kingdom of God is all about. They had started comparing their lists of "work accomplished" for God to see who the "best" disciple was. Can't you just see them? One would say that he was always there when Jesus needed anything. Another would say that they had been helping deliver meals to some people. Other disciples may comment on their giving to the ministry of Jesus. They were arguing over criteria centered on what they had done. Jesus needed

49

to reprioritize their thinking as to what are the most important things in this world.

To reveal to them the spiritual aspects of the Kingdom of God and who is greatest, Jesus had a little child stand beside Him. Jesus told them that they should welcome this little child in His name. What does this mean? Obviously, the first thing that the disciples had to do was to get their minds off themselves and what they were doing. Then, they had to open their eyes and ears to see the needs of children. This meant that the disciples had to place an extraordinary high value on children. This was the exact opposite of the value that society placed on children at the time of Christ.

But, I have to add that even today, most adults do not have much patience with children. That's a bold statement but it can be seen in how few of the older adults are willing to serve in some capacity in a children's ministry. It just seems that a lot of adults live with the understanding that they have done their work for children – it's time for others to work with children.

Jesus took their understanding of what makes someone great and turned it upside down. How do most people evaluate others as to who is greater than someone else? Is Mother Teresa greater in the Kingdom of heaven than my mother? Is Billy Graham greater in the Kingdom of heaven than my father?

Jesus uses the criteria of how we treat those who have nothing, who are defenseless, and who have been rejected by others. This is a huge jump from our current worldly thinking. Jesus makes it so important that He compares doing something for someone else in need the same as if you did it for Him. And, if you did it for Him, then you did it for God.

Check out your "criteria" on who will be the greatest in heaven. I am confident that it will be the people that we have not heard about or that we thought were insignificant. I think all of us could do with a little humility in what we do for others. We help those who need help without any recognition. We serve others as God puts people in our path who need a little encouragement. This is the Kingdom of God that the disciples (and we, today) have such a hard time visualizing because of our wrong perceptions of who is the greatest. Let this chapter be a wake-up call for you and how you serve others in the name of Christ.

17

JESUS

HE CAME ONCE AND HE'S
COMING AGAIN!

He who testifies to these things says, "Yes, I am coming
soon." Amen. Come, Lord Jesus. The grace of the Lord
Jesus be with God's people. Amen.

—REVELATION 22:20-21

AT CHRISTMAS WE CELEBRATE THE fact that God became a human being
in the flesh. The baby in the manger was God. He became like us to
walk a life that all of us walk. He was tempted and suffered in every way
that a human being could experience and more. He came so that He could
correct the wrongs that man has made. He came and died so that God's
required penalty for sin was paid in full with His death on the cross. He came
so that every single human being could have a healthy relationship with God.
He came to begin a spiritual work through the church, His people. He came
to give us life, and a life that is the most abundant that anyone can live on
this earth. These are just some of the reasons we celebrate His birth.

And, He's promised that He is coming again. This will be the final
chapter in man's long conflict with evil and Satan's battle against God.
His righteousness will defeat all of the forces of evil. He will remove sin,
death, Satan, and all of his demons from the presence of all Believers. He
will judge each person by the revelations that they have been given by God

to know who He is. He will judge all Believers on the spiritual work that each has done as a Believer in the name of Christ. He will create a new heaven and a new earth that will be our eternal home.

If you, as a Believer, would take the time to consider why He came the first time, your relationship with others would be based on the unconditional love that God showed you through His first coming. God desires that you love others as God has loved you. In this way, others can see and begin to understand why God came in the flesh. In the verses above, the response to the writer of the book of Revelation says, "Amen. Come, Lord Jesus." This should be the daily expectation of all Believers.

Also, in the verses above is the writer's request of God that, "The grace of the Lord Jesus be with God's people." You, as a Believer, need to review and renew your understanding of "grace" on a daily basis. Otherwise, the tendency is to take on the "gracelessness" of this world. And, I mean, the "gracelessness." You can see the ugliness of "gracelessness" when people mistreat you, when people's expectations of you are unrealistic, and, when you are not willing to forgive everyone in your life who has wronged you.

"Gracelessness" shows itself when we talk about others in a way to make sure that the person we are talking to has the same perspective that we have of how bad the others are. This is all too common because we feel like someone else should feel the same way about someone as we do. We do not want them to think good about that other person. Our goal is to make that person look bad. We actually get to the point where we want this person to feel bad, to hurt, and to be rejected by others. This is the ugliest of "gracelessness," and the opposite of unconditional love that God has for you.

Now, grace from God's perspective comes when we do something positive for someone who has done only wrong to us. This is impossible for any of us to do without knowing, understanding, and being humbled by the fact that Christ gave us grace. He gave us forgiveness of sins without us asking for forgiveness. The magnitude of His grace is like getting a million dollars while the grace that we give to others is only one dollar. And, yet, we will not give that dollar because of the way that person treats us. Jesus gave you more than a million dollars worth of grace. If you can comprehend that, then your giving of grace is motivated by the love Christ has for you. Result: lives will be changed and relationships restored.

With all of this in mind, just try to show someone else grace…giving something of value to someone who does not deserve it. It's at that time that the spiritual realm shouts "Amen" to the act of grace that you showed. We, as Believers, should respond with, "Amen, come Lord Jesus!"

18

GOD

HOW TO SEE HIM

Blessed are the pure in heart, for they will see God.

—MATTHEW 5:8

THE ABOVE VERSE IS PART of what is known as the Beatitudes in Matthew Chapter 5. Jesus is speaking to His disciples and, possibly, many others who were gathered around Him. He was telling them about what Believers are like in the Kingdom of God.

Probably, just like them, we have a hard time with the concept of a spiritual kingdom. Our world has so forced us to think of only what is in front of our faces. Or, even worse, not to accept anything unless you personally can see it, touch it, smell it, hear it, or figure it out for yourself. The wisdom of this world stands on the erroneous idea that there is nothing beyond our thinking. Unfortunately, most Christians, who have accepted the idea that unless they have experienced it then it didn't happen, have unknowingly and unintentionally defined "God" by the limits of their own thinking. In other words, if you live your life by the worldly wisdom of how "smart" a human being you are, then you cannot and will not be able to see God...even though He plainly reveals Himself in so many ways.

Jesus wanted to challenge His disciples (and us) to think beyond themselves...to get out of the "I want," "I need," "I deserve," "I've earned," and all of the other "self" defined behavior. He wanted them to see God!

53

Jesus' statement, "Blessed are the pure in heart, for they will see God," is the TRUTH about your natural and your spiritual life. All of us spend a lot of our time not being "pure in heart." We think of only ourselves. We think only what this world has done to us or what we have accomplished in this world. We plan what to say and how to react to manipulate others to feel a certain way toward us. "Pure in heart" is the opposite of this world. As Believers, we need to always realize that we live in a creation made by an all-powerful, all-knowing, all-encompassing God. We live in His creation. When we take our eyes off Him, our hearts become impure and we cannot see Him! It is spiritually impossible.

The Bible emphasizes that humility in service to others as being "pure in heart." This is what Jesus showed us while He lived among us as a human being. He never allowed the world to distract Him from the TRUTH about life. We look at His life while on earth and think that He could do it, because He is God. But, that's exactly the kind of life that God describes that people in His Kingdom live. And, that's the kind of life that God desires for every Believer to live in this world today. In this way, those who have been blinded by the philosophy of this world will see God at work in your life.

Jesus said that when you see Him, you see God. When you live "pure in heart," others will see Christ (God) in you. Strive every day to be "pure in heart," untainted by your own selfishness. You will live an entirely different life on this earth. You will see God and that is more wondrous than anything you could imagine for yourself. Jesus is the Way, the Truth, and the Life!

19

GOD

HIS WORD

For the word of God is living and active. Sharper than any
double-edged sword, it penetrates even to dividing soul
and spirit, joints and marrow; it judges the thoughts and
attitudes of the heart.

—HEBREWS 4:12

SOME PEOPLE BELIEVE THAT THERE is no God; therefore, there are no
words to hear or read about God. Unfortunately, many well-meaning
Christians either are unaware or forget that God's word is "living" and
"active" in their lives. All Believers struggle with the things of this world
crowding any thoughts of God out of their minds. If, as a Believer, you
do not intentionally think that God is working in your life each moment
of every day, it is easy to miss the words of God. The verse above is very
clear: His word is living and active.

It is so alive that things happen everyday in people's lives throughout
this entire world. Miracles occur where God's word is living and active.
Lives are changed when a person sees the TRUTH that comes from
hearing God's word. Do you anticipate God's word in your life every day?
That's how living and active His word is.

The verse goes on to say that God's word is "sharper than any double-
edged sword." I don't know about you, but I would not want to get hit by
a double edged sword as it would definitely cut my life in half. But that's

what God's word does to the "self" in you. God's word clearly says that we are to put to death those things that keep us from living the life that God intended. Jesus said that if anyone wanted to follow Him, they must pick up their cross daily.

So, when God's word is living and active in your life, the Holy Spirit will show you when you are being selfish and what changes are needed in your life to become more Christ-like. It will feel like a double-edged sword. Remember: it's not you doing the work but God's word. Read and study God's word to see this.

God's word also "penetrates even to dividing soul and spirit, joints and marrow." I pray that right now a thought comes to your mind that shows how self-oriented you are about something in your life. We are talking about the deeper thoughts and motives that only you can know about as God's word reveals who you really are.

Now, if and when these deeper selfish thoughts and motives come to your mind, the Holy Spirit through God's word is there to "judge the thoughts and attitudes" of your heart. And, guess what the first thing you will do is? Deny, justify, and lie to yourself that you are not that selfish. But it is God's word that is living and active that is showing you these things. By denying this "judgment" you set yourself up higher than the authority of God. In essence, you are telling God that you know what is best for you. It is at these moments that God brings His word to you to say that He loves you and has the best in mind for you.

Again, watch carefully for that deceitful "self" that you have. That "self" in you will never come under the authority of God. But, when you humbly read and hear His word, there is a spiritual energy that cannot compare to anything on this earth. God's power through the Holy Spirit will so fill your life that you will not want anything but Him. Read, study, and hear His word today that is prepared just for you and just for today!

20

GOD

HE IS GOD

All the peoples of the earth are regarded as nothing. He does as he pleases with the powers of heaven and the peoples of the earth. No one can hold back his hand or say to him: "What have you done?"

—DANIEL 4:35

WELL, THIS VERSE IS A real "pick me up," isn't it? You and I and everyone else are regarded as nothing. A statement like that does not do much for your self esteem or your ego. But that's probably the key to this verse. Has mankind gotten to the point that it is all about "us" and not God?

I don't know any other way of saying it: God is in control! God is sovereign! God is God! Early in my life when I was establishing a career and trying to make money, I really and truly believed that it was all about how hard I worked and who I knew and who I could impress to get ahead in this world. All of my personal efforts to make a life for myself (and every now and then for my family) came to a crashing halt when I reached a point where I realized I was nothing in this world. This world is so complex and so unpredictable all because it is under the rule of Satan. I never thought of that. I was just "tooling" along trying to make the best of things when one day, I realized that I was messing things up royally.

Oh, I was a Christian. I had no doubts that my relationship to God was all because of the blood of Christ and nothing of myself. But, I did not spend much time thinking of the "spiritual" side of living. I had a world to conquer! Oh, how deceived I was. The Bible describes such a life: no peace, no joy, no freedom, and no true relationships with others. Then, I realized that God is God! He existed, exists, and will exist for eternity. Me…I'm here today and gone tomorrow.

Jesus as the WAY, the TRUTH, and the LIFE became very real to me. The WAY to live life on this earth is only through a healthy relationship with God made possible by the death and resurrection of Jesus Christ. This WAY can be lived only by the power that raised Jesus from the dead: the Holy Spirit.

The TRUTH became clearer as I discovered that the goals and priorities of a worldly life are never achievable. I was told by many people early in my life that I had it "made" because of my personal success. Hogwash! God removed me from all of those "human" successes to show me the TRUTH. The world deceives. There is no true peace, joy, and success in this world. Once you have achieved what you think is success, the world changes the rules.

The LIFE is constantly striving to live the same life that Christ (God) lived on this earth. Jesus did only what God told Him to do. He was always doing the will of the Father. Sometimes it did not look like it; but, here comes the other part of the verse above. God does as He pleases! He has sacrificed Himself to restore a relationship with every man, woman, and child. God loves us! He desires fellowship with us! He willingly sacrificed everything to have that relationship. He does as He pleases!

I don't know about you but I'm glad God is who He says He is. He does as He pleases with the powers of heaven and the peoples of the earth. He knows what He is doing. I am so glad that He brought me to the most humbling and empty point in my life so that I could see that He is God!

Examine the past and see what your priorities were and are. Don't deceive yourself. Be honest. Focus on this verse and compare it to your life. You are nothing and God is everything. Your real value comes from living a life for God. This will definitely change your life.

21

YOUR LIFE
GOD'S FEET AND MOUTH

"Ah, Sovereign LORD," I said, "I do not know how to
speak; I am only a child." But the LORD said to me, "Do
not say, 'I am only a child.' You must go to everyone I
send you to and say whatever I command you. Do not be
afraid of them, for I am with you and will rescue you,"
declares the LORD.

—JEREMIAH 1:6-8

THE VERSES ABOVE COME FROM God's call on the life of Jeremiah. What
interested me about these verses is that I think they speak to every
Believer living today. Jesus told His disciples to go into all the world and
make disciples. This statement was said to ALL Believers!

What is also very interesting is Jeremiah's response to God's call: "I
am only a child." This sounds just like something that we would say. We
don't know what to tell people about the things of God. Our thoughts are:
"What if I say the wrong thing?" "What will they think of me?" "I'll be
called a religious fanatic." "I'll lose them as my friends." And on and on
with excuses. The problem is that our focus is on us and what others will
think of us. We do not consider the ETERNAL aspect of the God of all
creation leading us to say something to someone else that impacts their
eternal life. I hope that by the time you have read this, you have a different
view of why your life is so important to God.

The verses above also say that God will send you to the people that need Him. WOW!! What an awesome realization this was for my life! It finally dawned on me that I did not work where I was employed for me to make money or to have a career. It was God who put me in the various work positions with others to be available for God to use me. There were so many times when someone would come to me to ask a question about the things of God in the workplace. One person that I recall would eat lunch with me once or twice a week to talk about "things." As it turned out, he was having an affair that was causing serious relationship problems with his wife and children. God gave me the words to speak.

Interestingly, God wanted me to talk only of Him, not the man's messed up life. Time after time, I spoke of God's love, forgiveness, and grace. I never judged the man as being right or wrong in what he was doing. He eventually divorced his wife and moved in with this other woman. But, I continued to talk to him about God, Christ, and the Holy Spirit. Time passed and he took a job in another company and I retired, so we lost contact. However, he called me one day to tell me he had accepted Christ and asked me if I would come to his church for his baptism. He had also started dating his ex-wife and eventually, they remarried. His eternal life is different because someone took the time (and a long time at that) to tell him about God.

God has placed you with others so that He can speak through you. It could be a neighbor, people on a tennis court or golf course, people where you work, and many others. All Believers should see their lives as God sees them…to serve an eternal purpose in reflecting God's love and forgiveness to others. 99.9% of the people you come in contact with want to see someone who has strong convictions about God, Christ, and the Holy Spirit as opposed to what you should or should not be doing. After all, it is the Holy Spirit that leads people to God, not you.

God also says not to be afraid, because He will be with you and rescue you. I can see that God is with Believers wherever they are and in whatever they are doing. But what about this word "rescue"? Are our lives threatened when we speak of the things of God? YES! Jesus spoke only what God the Father told Him to say and His life was very much threatened. But, God rescued Him by His resurrection through the power of the Holy Spirit. And, amazingly, the Bible says that by that same Spirit, God will raise you up. So, where does the fear come from when talking to others about God? It comes from the "flesh" that is in us.

May I suggest that you focus on the sovereignty of God. Ask the Holy Spirit to "remind" you that you are where God wants you for an eternal purpose. Also, ask the Holy Spirit to "remind" you that the eternity of God is many times more significant than one little conversation where someone may get upset with you because you told them about God. Remember, it is not you that they are rejecting but God who is revealing Himself through what you say about Him.

22

YOUR LIFE
IMITATE GOD?

Be imitators of God, therefore, as dearly loved children and
live a life of love, just as Christ loved us and gave himself
up for us as a fragrant offering and sacrifice to God.

—EPHESIANS 5:1-2

Is THIS POSSIBLE?!! Is IT possible that a human being living on this sin-filled world can imitate God? This sounds so impossible!

Although this is one of my favorite verses, it continues to be one of the most challenging for me. Just think that as a Believer, God intends for you to live your life on this earth as Christ did. In both the Old Testament and the New Testament, God's Word says for us to be "as holy as God/Christ is holy." WOW!! If you think about this, it is astounding that a fleshy human being could imitate God. How can this be?!!

It seems impossible because of how we think of who God is. God is above and beyond anything that any person could think of. He is Spirit while we are flesh. He is everything that you could possibly imagine for describing something that exists, and that's just the starting point. He is all that exists and is the cause of all that exists. Do you get the idea of how astounding it is that He says to Believers, "Imitate Me"? How?

Well, one way not to imitate God is, unfortunately, how most Believers attempt to live a life imitating God. We do it by using our own flesh. We are driven to obtain our own self-worth through worldly actions and achievements.

What this means is that we try to be nice to people we don't like. We try to be happy when things are bad. We don't want others to know about some of the dirty laundry lying around in our lives. And, read this carefully, we are very concerned about what others think about us. If it is other Believers, then we want to appear spiritual; if we are around non-Believers, we want to fit in. This is the major problem with Christians today, because you really can't tell the difference between a Believer and a non-Believer. Both are doing what, and listen to this carefully, "they think" it takes to obtain self-worth. As Believers, those things that we identify as giving us self-worth easily become our "idols", and we look just like everyone else in this world. We substitute a relationship with God to maintain our idols. We are deceived!

In the verses above, God tells us how to imitate Him. Live your life every day knowing that God loves you unconditionally. This is the source for the deepest and most genuine "worth" of a person. Knowing you are loved just as you are frees you up from all of the facades and hypocrisy that makes your life miserable here on earth. Love God and love others. But, how? That's the challenge of these verses and, He tells us how in these verses: "...just as Christ loved you and gave Himself up for you!" Instead of your trying to live a Christian life through your flesh, allow the Holy Spirit to show you how Christ imitated God while He (Christ) was on earth. Jesus offered Himself as an offering and a sacrifice to God. Give up on trying to live the life that you have mapped out in your head and give yourself to the love of God.

Now, I know some of you are still asking, "How?" If you are still wondering "how," then you are still trying to figure out how "YOU" can imitate God. Stop it!

Consider this: God as a Spirit became a human being (Jesus) to sacrifice Himself so that you can have a relationship with God. That's why God created us: to have a relationship with Him. I repeat: God became like you and me, so that through His sacrifice we would become like Him. Therefore, a Believer relies on only God (Christ and the Holy Spirit) to imitate God. It's allowing God to live through your life.

When you live your life as a Believer by the power of the Holy Spirit (and not by your own power), your life will reveal the deepest need of human beings – to be loved unconditionally. By presenting yourself as a living sacrifice to God, your life is raised to the highest level of human existence – to be a child of God. Living your life as a Believer by your own thinking will result in a very tired, worn out, and disillusioned Believer. Living your life as a Believer by knowing God's unconditional love for you allows you to love others just as they are. That's how Believers can imitate God and become a sweet fragrance to Him.

23

YOUR LIFE
GUARD YOUR MIND

Then they understood that he was not telling them to
guard against the yeast used in bread, but against the
teaching of the Pharisees and Sadducees.

—MATTHEW 16:12

IT IS AMAZING TO ME how I thought about things before I began to
understand that God wanted me to be a "living sacrifice" to Him. I
definitely had 30 years of the world in my mind. I had bought into the
world with its values and philosophies. I'm not blaming the world for my
lifestyle; it was always my choice on how to live. The problem was that I
had most of my focus on me and not God and others.

In the verse above, the Pharisees and Sadducees were not living their
lives based on God's Word even though they read and studied the Old
Testament. Note: at the time of Jesus, the "Old Testament" was called the
Tanakh or Hebrew Bible. The word "Tanakh" is like an acrostic for the three
categories of the books of the Hebrew Bible: the <u>T</u>orah ("Instructions"),
the <u>N</u>evi'im ("Prophets"), and the <u>K</u>etuvim ("Writings"). The Hebrew
Bible is virtually the same as our Old Testament with variations in the
order of the books.

The Jewish leaders had reached a level of knowledge that, interestingly,
describes the worldly philosophies of today: yeast. They were what you
would call "legalists." Their being "right" about things was the driving

force on how they lived their lives. What they did was considered as "righteous" by man, but not by Christ. It was all about who they were and what they did. Since they were in a position of authority and power, their "right way of living" greatly influenced the Jews at that time. Once this philosophy of "self righteousness" gets a start in a person, it is like yeast in dough - it expands taking up more space in the pan (your mind).

In the verse above, it appears that Jesus was making a contrast between bread of this earth and the bread of heaven. Jesus quoted Deuteronomy when He was tempted by Satan to turn stones into bread. He told Satan that man did not live by earthly bread alone but by the spiritual bread that is the Word of God. He equated the Word of God with spiritual bread.

Many times, Believers have heard sermons on the Bible being the daily bread for Christians to grow in their spiritual relationship with God. Can you see the significance of Jesus' comment above that was directed to His disciples? On numerous occasions, He saw a lack of spiritual understanding and growth with His disciples. He said they had little faith. He even asked Himself why He had to continue to put up with them.

God can be asking the same of us today. We will willingly read a "spiritual" book about God or Christ or anything related to Christianity. But, to read and study the Bible itself becomes tedious and boring. We say we don't understand so we leave the spiritual bread of life to go to the bread of this earth.

There are some great books written to help us understand the Bible or to offer us encouragement or to help us grow spiritually. The books of C. S. Lewis are some of my favorite. I've read *Mere Christianity* numerous times. Have you ever thought that you would meet C. S. Lewis in heaven? However, I don't think you will find any of his books there. In heaven, we will have the truth from the Source of Truth. The Bible is God's Word for us living on earth today.

As we try to figure out how to guard our minds in this world, we need to realize that we are in Satan's territory or, as one theologian put it, "enemy-occupied territory." This should always keep us on guard for the yeast of this world. TV, books, and movies are being used intentionally to bring people to a point that "anything goes" as long as you are comfortable and happy. These things encourage the redefinition of marriage that is not God's definition. These things encourage men to become involved in pornography, destroying relationships with their spouses and others. These things present a picture that women's appearance (cosmetics, clothing, and accessories) determines their personal self-worth. Beauty is all on the outside as opposed to God's Word that says that God looks on the heart - the beauty inside not outside.

I could go on and on, but every effort by us to use the yeast we get from worldly acceptable standards is a wasted effort because the end result is always broken relationships, personal turmoil, and, worst of all, no real meaningful purpose for living life. Turn off the TV and read God's Word. Make God's Word a daily part of your life so that spiritual nourishment gives you peace and a true purpose for your life.

24

HOLY SPIRIT
YOUR GUARANTEE FROM GOD

Do not cast me from your presence or take your Holy Spirit from me. Restore to me the joy of your salvation and grant me a willing spirit, to sustain me.

—PSALM 51:11-12

THE VERSES ABOVE COME FROM Psalm 51 written by King David after he had been convicted of his sins. David had committed adultery with another man's wife; tried to cover it up when the woman became pregnant; and, with all moral restraint gone, had her husband killed. We would consider these some serious violations of our current laws as well as the Ten Commandments. So, what was going on with David? For most of his life, David lived in the Spirit. But, he got comfortable and stopped thinking about God and set his heart on the things of this earth.

The consequences of David's living in the flesh were death - the death of the baby that was a result of his being with the other man's wife. After David acknowledged his sins before God, he asked God to allow him to keep the Holy Spirit. In the Old Testament times, the Holy Spirit would come and go. David knew that the Holy Spirit could leave him and he knew that it was the Spirit that gave him the power to do the work of God. David faced the same choices that we have today: either live in the flesh or live in the Spirit.

Everyday, all Believers make this same decision: flesh or Spirit. God has given all Believers the Holy Spirit to live within us forever. Jesus said that He must leave this earth so that the Holy Spirit would come and live in Believers. Jesus said the Holy Spirit would be the power to transform our lives from our worldly flesh to become more like Him on this earth. Paul said that the Holy Spirit was a deposit guaranteeing our future salvation through Jesus Christ. God said that He raised Jesus from the dead through the power of the Holy Spirit and that He would do the same for us through the power of the Holy Spirit. The bottom line to all of this is that a Believer can do nothing of himself and that God provides the Holy Spirit to empower the Believer. David realized the power of the Holy Spirit and did not want to lose it.

Most Believers today live their lives without ever considering the POWER of the Holy Spirit. We should all be like David in always remembering that God has given us the Holy Spirit. Although the power of the Holy Spirit is ALWAYS with the Believer, just like David we have to choose to live in faith by thinking of God's love, grace, and forgiveness provided through Jesus Christ; then, the power of the Spirit will enable us to do the work of God.

The weakness of Christians to live a life worthy of Christ is all because Christians rely on their flesh to try to be like Christ. Non-believers quickly see the hypocrisy in this. With the current worldly philosophy of "you do whatever you want as long it does not hurt someone else," we Believers have become impotent in our witness for the power of God in our lives. Others say, "Go ahead and live the way you want, but don't bother me with it." Our lives as Believers should be a daily walk knowing that God has placed the Holy Spirit in our lives. We should live out the joy, regardless of the circumstances, given to us by God because He has given us everything we need to live a holy life on this earth. We will not face the wrathful judgment of God because of Christ's death and resurrection.

These should be our daily thoughts. And, when we focus on those things of God, the Holy Spirit provides the power to live a life that has an eternal purpose and significance. Your life will be different resulting in the fruit of the Spirit: love, joy, peace, patience, kindness, goodness, faithfulness, gentleness and self-control. WOW!! What a life to live in the middle of all of the chaos, confusion, animosity, and fear that is in the world today. Just like David, you can choose to live based on your own "life stuff" or you can forget about yourself and focus on the "new life" that God has given you. Then, the Holy Spirit will empower you beyond anything you can imagine.

25

GOD

HIS TESTIMONY

> In the past, he let all nations go their own way. Yet he
> has not left himself without testimony: He has shown
> kindness by giving you rain from heaven and crops in their
> seasons; he provides you with plenty of food and fills your
> hearts with joy.
>
> —ACTS 14:16-17

THE VERSES ABOVE RESULTED WHEN some people tried to claim that Paul and Barnabas were "gods." The people started to worship them. Of course, Paul and Barnabas denied this and tried to point the people to God and Christ. The verses above are the heart of their reply - God's testimony of who He is.

God, in His sovereignty, has permitted nations and people to go their own way. When they forgot about God, He would "judge" them through hardships to remember who He is. As human beings, we don't like judgment (unless we are doing the judging). Yet, every time God judged, He demonstrated His grace toward us. This is His testimony to us.

For example, God judged Adam and Eve by removing them from the Garden of Eden when they disobeyed Him. He showed His grace in this judgment because He did not want them to eat of the "tree of life" and live forever in their sinful condition always trying to hide from God. This is His testimony to us.

For example, God judged the entire earth when everyone did everything of their own imagination with no thought for God. He showed His grace when He saved Noah and his family with the building of an ark (boat) to wait out the flooding of the earth. He put the rainbow in the sky as a reminder of His testimony to us.

For example, God utterly destroyed Sodom and Gomorrah and all of their inhabitants because of their rebellion against God. He showed His grace when He sent two angels to bring Lot and his family out of those cities before He destroyed them. This is His testimony to us.

The ultimate example is when God judged our sins by putting that judgment onto Christ as He was crucified. He showed His grace when He forgave all of our sins through the blood sacrifice of Christ on the cross. This is His testimony to us.

So, God lets us go our own way until our rebellion reaches a point of judgment. He will remove Believers from this judgment because of the death and resurrection of Christ. This is His testimony of who He is that comes through His grace and His judgment.

In the verses above, it also describes the testimony of God through the kindness that He has shown us. As Believers, He has surrounded us with His protection and nothing can get to us without His permission. He has provided us everything we need to live a "godly" life here on earth. He has given us the Holy Spirit whose power raised Jesus from the dead. He has allowed us to see Him at work through others providing us joy in our hearts to which nothing in this world can compare.

With all of this in mind, what do you think God's testimony is today to human beings? Your life! Jesus said that your life is lived to its fullest when you love God with everything you have and you love others as yourself. This "living sacrifice" for God and others results in having a clear purpose for your life. You live with meaning as you serve others. Allow the Holy Spirit to show you those areas in your life that need to be refocused onto God and others. God's testimony = your life. Your life = God's testimony. What does your life look like to others?

26

YOU

ARE THE TEMPLE OF

THE HOLY SPIRIT

> This is what the Lord Almighty says: "These people say, 'The time has not yet come for the Lord's House to be built.'" Then the word of the Lord came through the prophet Haggai: "Is it a time for you yourselves to be living in your paneled houses, while this house remains a ruin?"
>
> —HAGGAI 1:2-4

THE VERSES ABOVE COME FROM a Minor Prophet, Haggai, but they speak volumes to us as Believers today. The situation described in these verses occurred when the Jewish temple in Jerusalem was to be rebuilt around 520 B.C. Approximately seventy years before Haggai had written theses words, the temple had been destroyed and the people deported to Babylon. Seventy years later, the Mede-Persia King Cyrus allowed the Jews to return to rebuild their temple. They had started to rebuild the temple in 536 B.C., but became more focused on living their own lives and taking care of their own houses. God asked, "Is it a time for you yourselves to be living in your paneled houses, while this house remains a ruin?"

Now, these verses could be related to the physical condition of church buildings today regardless of denomination. But, I want to get more specific in applying these verses to your life. If you are wondering what this has to do with your life as a Believer, then understand that in the New Testament, God sent the Holy Spirit to dwell within you. In other words, and the Bible puts it this way, your body is the temple of the Holy Spirit. What condition is your body in today?

I am not only speaking about your physical body, but also your heart, mind, and soul. As a Believer, your entire being has been made new by the power of the Holy Spirit. This means your heart, mind, and soul should be going through a process of "building" toward being Christlike. This building process is called "sanctification." Sanctification is an ongoing and life-long process of changing our behavior, attitudes, values, and decisions to be based on God's perspective and not our worldly perspective. This is your entire being. As you grow in grace and knowledge of our Lord Jesus Christ on a daily basis, you will be made conformed to the image of Christ. In other words, people will see Christ through who you are.

But, if you are not investing the time and energy to your "building" as a Believer, your Believer's life will be in ruins. Ruins can be seen as relationships that are broken, a peace that seems just out of reach, a busyness about your life that leaves you exhausted, and no hope in the future. Your worldly life may look good (for a little while), but everything in this world corrodes, rots, gets dirty, has to be maintained, etc. When you invest in eternal things, your life becomes full and complete with purpose.

There is another way of looking at the verses from Haggai. The Bible says that each Believer makes up the body of Christ. Each of us has received a spiritual gift that we are to use to encourage others. The body of Christ is most powerful when all of the members are applying their gift in loving God and serving others. A local church has many members, but they do not have the same gifts. What this means is that God has placed you where you are in the body of Christ for a spiritual purpose. If your spiritual building is in ruins, then that part of the body of Christ is not as powerful.

God intends for all Believers to be involved in His Kingdom. This happens when we get our minds off ourselves, off our homes, off of the things of this world, and put it on God. We should first think of God and His Son, Jesus Christ, dying on the cross with every moment of our lives. We should think of the resurrection of Christ through the same power that is in you – the Holy Spirit. This is how you "build" your spiritual life and live a life by the Spirit. We are all in the same process.

Therefore, make your spiritual life something that you become intentional about building. Don't make it just on Sundays, or it will be in ruins. Live the life that God purposed for you through the Holy Spirit that He gave you as a guarantee for all of His promises.

27

GOD

HE IS ACTIVE IN TODAY'S WORLD EVENTS

> Then Daniel praised the God of heaven and said: "Praise be to the name of God for ever and ever; wisdom and power are his. He changes times and seasons; he sets up kings and deposes them. He gives wisdom to the wise and knowledge to the discerning. He reveals deep and hidden things; he knows what lies in darkness, and light dwells with him."
>
> —DANIEL 2:19B-22

PRAISING GOD FOR BEING ACTIVE in today's world events should be part of every Believer's daily life. When he saw the work of God in the world, Daniel proclaimed praise to God for ever and ever: never-ending praise because of what God does in this world. As Believers, we should be like Daniel; but, we can only truly praise God when, by faith, we acknowledge His work in this world and in our lives.

When you think of someone wise, do you think of God? Wisdom comes only from God. Wisdom is how you apply the knowledge that you have obtained. The smartest people in the world may not be very wise. Wisdom is based on who God is, not what this world thinks of wisdom. The world thinks a wise person is someone who invests money and gets a high rate of return. God's wisdom involves people and relationships. God wants you to know who He is and then apply that knowledge to the people involved in your life. Wisdom is exercised when you forgive someone who has wronged you unjustly. Wisdom is used when you are no longer worldly minded but eternally minded. Wisdom sees the needs of other people and how to minister to those people based on the love of God. You may be one of the wisest people in the world when you deny yourself and serve others.

When you see the awesome power in nature or in the universe, do you think of God? When you know, by faith, that God is all powerful, you give up yourself and trust in God. God's power is manifested in the work of the Holy Spirit. The power of the Holy Spirit raised Jesus from the dead. The power of the Holy Spirit now resides in each Believer. When God's power is used, the finite is turned upside down by the infinite. Everything in this world pales to the awesome power of the God who created the universe and everything in it. Believers mature when they reach a point in their lives that they realize everything was created by Him and for Him and that everything holds together because of Him. (Colossians 1:17)

In the verses above, Daniel reminds us of how God works in our world on a daily basis. If you think of someone inventing Daylight Saving Time, then think of God as creating all "times" and seasons. God knew we would be bored if there was no past, present, or future. He knew we would vegetate if there were no changes in the seasons. All of us get a little excited if we hear that there is snow in a forecast. God controls the times and seasons we experience on earth.

God also controls who is in control (or, at least, think they are in control). This world is currently under the dominion of Satan and his demons. But, right now, Satan and his demons are living on borrowed time. When Christ died and was resurrected, Satan lost the war. He knows his time is short and he is doing everything he can to destroy people's lives through broken relationships. Satan can do nothing without God's ok. Therefore, whoever is elected to political office, whoever runs a company, whoever becomes an influential person, whoever becomes your supervisor at work...all of these people are there for God's purpose. Sometimes it is to bless and sometimes it is to judge, but in all things, "God is in control!"

If you find yourself fretting over the condition of your country, consider this quote: "I tremble for my country when I reflect that God is just." - Thomas Jefferson, 1781, just five years after the signing of the Declaration of Independence. What did Thomas Jefferson see over 200 years ago that could be the same thought that many of us have about our nation today? Don't put your faith in a country of this temporal world; put your faith in the God of eternity.

God reveals the deep and hidden things. You know what these things are. When you read the previous paragraph, you may have thought "why" God would allow such and such. The deep and hidden things are the reasons that God allows things to happen on this earth. Many people do not accept that Jesus Christ was the Son of God, that He died on the cross, that His blood covers all of our sins, and that He was resurrected. If you do accept Christ, then realize that God will reveal deep and hidden things... but, only when you are fully engaged with God. He doesn't reveal things because we have to know why. He reveals things for His eternal purposes. When He reveals those eternal purposes to us, we will fall down and praise him with all of our being.

Finally, light dwells with God. I don't think this is the light we see when we flip a switch. This is spiritual light. This is the light that shines from us to others when we deny ourselves and look on others as better than ourselves. This is the light that gives us direction for our lives so that we are involved in the relationships that God has chosen. This is the light that allows us to look at others and see the eternal need that they have in their life to either accept Christ or grow spiritually. Whether you are down and out or higher than a kite, praise God!

28

YOU

ARE CREATED SPECIAL BY GOD

I praise you because I am fearfully and wonderfully made;
your works are wonderful, I know that full well.

—PSALM 139:14

YOU ARE A SPECIAL CREATION created by God. Your life is of immense value, because God's Son died for you. God has a plan for your life that is unique to you. Your life has an eternal meaning and purpose for God to use for His honor and glory. When you live a life seeing the value that God places on you, your life is full and abundant.

Unfortunately, our lives today have become of less value than God intended.

Movies, TV shows, and computer games have made the killing and destroying of people part of the "entertainment" in our lives. Teens cannot wait for the next computer game that increases the "realness" of what they are playing. Children are exposed to innumerable images of dead people and they begin to draw pictures of death, skulls and bones, etc. When people play computer games that kill and destroy others for fun, then, life, as God intended, becomes of less value. Life becomes cheap. Those teens and children grow up and begin to think about their own value. If they try to get it from the world, they end up with a life that has no meaning or purpose. Everything turns sour when we try to get something from this world.

Abortion is a cheap way to destroy a life that is not wanted. Our country has passed laws that make abortion legal. Abortion makes the creation of life a human decision and not God's. Can you see the arrogance and audacity of "man" to come to a point where "man" decides on life? "Man" cannot handle this decision. "Man" cannot handle anything that God has created. We think we can learn enough and become smart enough to "control" and manage things that God has created. However, the history of man's decisions has proven that we don't know what we are doing. God will judge this country and others on taking the decision of creating life away from God.

On a positive note, I find it astonishing, and I am in awe when I consider God creating you and me. Take a moment to think about how your body functions. Think of your eyes that can see everything at a glance. Without eyes, you could not see light (another of God's creations). Think of your ears and the complexity of tiny bones that enable you to hear. Amazing! Think of your digestive system that houses some of the most lethal bacteria in the world but does not destroy your body while it digests everything that you eat. Unbelievable!

The life that God has given you is not just the physical. You are very special because God made you in His image. You can think, reason, have emotions, and make decisions, because God desired a creation that would desire to have a relationship with Him. This is a choice that every single human being makes during their life. Is there a God? Does He care for me? Does He have a plan for my life? The answer for all of these questions is "Yes!" Each person gets to decide if their life will be dedicated to God or to this world. That's the choice God has given you and each moment of each day gives you an opportunity to remember who you are from God's point of view and not the world's.

Thank Him for the life that He has created in you. Your life is unique, because God has planned things in your life that will cause you to turn to Him. As you live a life of gratitude to God, others will see the results in your life that are in stark contrast to this world. The value of life for everyone will become important to you. You will not take advantage of others. You will forgive others quickly and look for ways to invest valuable things that you own into their life so that they will see Christ in you. Your life will be full of peace and joy because you know that God created you, and He created you for a purpose. You and I are fearfully and wonderfully made. This should make you want to praise God right now!

29

YOUR LIFE
FOCUSED ON CHRIST

What is more, I consider everything a loss compared to the
surpassing greatness of knowing Christ Jesus my Lord, for
whose sake I have lost all things. I consider them rubbish,
that I may gain Christ, and be found in him, not having
a righteousness of my own that comes from the law, but
that which is through faith in Christ – righteousness that
comes from God and is by faith.

—PHILIPPIANS 3:8-9

PAUL WROTE THESE WORDS AS a summary of his life after he had accepted Jesus Christ as his Lord and Savior. These verses are extremely difficult to live out in our lives today as Believers in the USA. We desire everything in our lives today to be a gain. We always want to be on the positive side of obtaining wealth.

Consider those people who track the stock market on a daily basis. They are driven to always be gaining. When the market declines, they begin to panic and do everything they can to reduce the loss. What do you think Paul's perspective of the stock market would be? Suppose Paul invested in the market and experienced a loss. I tend to think that it would not bother him in the least bit, because his life's focus was on Christ. He would call his loss "rubbish." I know some of you are saying, "But that's my life savings!" Read those words again and ask how your life is saved.

It is saved by the sacrifice of Christ on the cross, not by how much money you have in a portfolio of stocks.

Another aspect of our lives today is the market value of our homes. Only in America could the perceived value of your home dictate your value in society. The bigger, the fancier, and the more landscaped your home is, the "wealthier" you will appear to others. If Paul owned one of those houses, how would he view it? He would probably down-size to fit his lifestyle. (In his case, it would likely be a tent.) Read the verses above again and you will find Paul considering his house as no longer a possession of his. There is nothing wrong about anyone's house and the cost of that house. There is something wrong if we have set our hearts on appearing "well-off" because of our homes. Our hearts should be focused on Christ and those things in heaven, not the things of this earth.

And then there's the property that our house sits on. We want to make sure that our neighbors are cutting their grass on time, not putting their garbage cans out too early, keeping up the appearance of the neighborhood, not painting their house school bus yellow. Why? Because our focus is on our property value; we don't want it to decrease but increase. Paul would not be worried about those things because he is thinking of his heavenly home. He is thinking of his eternal life to be lived with God. It doesn't matter if your neighbor plants some bushes on your property line or even on your property. God would consider your relationship with that neighbor of higher value than those bushes. You can do this only if you consider everything you have and own as rubbish, so that you may know Christ. You will be exercising your faith by keeping a healthy relationship with your neighbors so that they will see Christ in you.

Not only do we place an inordinate value on our property, we also place the wrong value on what is inside of our homes. When we purchase carpet and furnishings to make our home look good, we do not want our children, or the neighborhood kids, or our grandchildren to ruin any of our "stuff." We read the "riot act" to our children to keep them from ruining our "stuff." I don't think Paul would mind if any child spilled something on the carpet in his home. I don't think Paul would get upset if children tracked muddy shoes into his house. His focus was on knowing more about Christ. May I suggest that we need to remember that children are like the "Kingdom of God." It would surprise you how much children can teach us about the things of God, if we would give up protecting and worrying over our earthly possessions and spend more time with children.

Finally, our righteousness does not come from anything on this earth.

This is probably the most abused term for us as Believers. We want to place a self- righteous value based on the things we do or we possess on this earth (like the things discussed above). Listen! There is nothing on this earth that will make you righteous. Your most righteous work on this earth should be considered as rubbish. That's what Paul thought about all of his "good deeds." Our righteousness comes from God alone and is given to us freely by the work of Christ on the cross, when He died for all of our sins. This should be the focus of our lives, as Believers, on this earth. Others will see the faith you have when you consider everything about you as nothing. It will take faith to "give up" the stock market, your home, your property, and your furnishings. Others will take a second look at you when you don't get upset at losing any value in these earthy items. They will want to know how you do it. That's the eternal purpose that God has for your life: to tell others what Christ has done for you.

30

YOUR LIFE

GOD HAS A PLAN

"For I know the plans I have for you," declares the Lord, "plans to prosper you and not to harm you, plans to give you hope and a future."

—JEREMIAH 29:11

THIS VERSE GIVES SUCH A peace about life. Just think that God, who created everything, has plans for you! I know personally that we would like to believe that we are in control of our own destiny. Oh, we try to figure out God's will for our lives but usually we have already made up our minds and all we want is a rubber stamp of approval from God. God's plans for your life are to bring you to a point of accepting Him and to be a witness to others for Him.

God's ultimate desire is that every person will believe in Him - that everyone will choose Jesus Christ as their Savior and Lord. The plans God has for your life is to satisfy that desire. However, God gave us a free will to reject Him. I say it this way, because I believe that everyone who is born has their name written in the Book of Life. This is the book that God looks at to determine who will live with Him in heaven. The names of all babies and children are in that book. The names of all adults are not.

What happens during a person's life is that God has planned events that will cause that person to think of God. God will repeatedly reveal Himself to each and every person. These are some of the plans that God has for everyone. Eventually, each person will accept or reject God's revelation. If they consciously and intentionally reject God's revelation to them, then God removes their name from the Book of Life. Therefore, some of God's plans are all about you having God reveal Himself to you in a way that is special and unique for you.

When you reach the point of accepting God's revelations and become a Believer, God has some new and different plans for your life. These plans are to position your life in such a way that you will become more Christ-like in your attitudes and behavior. God wants this because your life becomes a living testimony for Him. Others will see Christ in you and want to know more about God.

The verse above is exciting, because God says that He has plans to prosper you. We all like to prosper! I don't think that God means wealth from the world's point of view. I think God is saying that the life you have knowing Him will be full and abundant from a spiritual perspective. Your life will definitely be prosperous when you consider that you are a co-heir with Christ in God's Kingdom. He also says that He has plans not to harm you. This involves God's judgment of our sins. Christ paid the price for our sins on the cross. Therefore, those of us who trust in the work of Christ will not suffer separation from God because of our sins.

God also has plans to give us a hope and a future. As already mentioned above, we will be co-heirs with Christ. We will also live an eternal life with God. God's original plan for us as human beings was to have an eternal relationship with Him. Our sins destroy that relationship. Because of His work to restore a right relationship with us, we will live with Him eternally. At some time in the future, our bodies will be resurrected and changed into a glorified body that will never grow old and die. WOW!!

So, you can create your own plans for your life without God and, I believe, they will fail. You may reach a worldly goal through your plans, but you will not have the basis for a truly contented life. Your life will be purposeless and hopeless. Only through the TRUTH about life will a person understand the true meaning of life. God has plans for you to discover that true meaning of life. When you do discover it, you'll wonder why you waited so long.

31

WISDOM
COMES FROM GOD

If any of you lacks wisdom, he should ask God, who gives generously to all without finding fault, and it will be given to him.

—JAMES 1:5

EVERYONE KNOWS THAT THE SMARTEST people on earth are teenagers. It's amazing how much they know that you don't know. It is also amazing how they know how to operate any machinery, perform any and all tasks, and can do anything without any help. My son went through this stage. I remember trying to show him something for the first time, but he said he already knew it. He also considered me not very smart during his teen years. Someone has said that when teens turn 20, they are amazed at how much their parents learned while they were teenagers.

The world considers "smartness" as how much education a person has. We consider people smart if they have a PhD. We think lawyers and medical doctors are smart because of what they know. People who do research have to be smart because they are on the leading edge of knowledge. The thing about all of this "smartness" is that it always involves facts. It involves what a person has learned and retained in their brain. For example, someone smart in religion will be able to give the Hebrew and Greek meanings to words in our Bible. The ultimate smart person is the one who reads all the books ever written and is able to recall their contents. This has not been done!

Most people don't have wisdom because knowledge is so highly valued in the world today. The world's motto could be, "Get smart...get knowledge." Today, people love to learn about the facts about things. This is a result of our dependence on reason and logic. It also shows man's arrogance, because we really and truly believe that we are capable of knowing everything. We say that there is a reason for everything; we just haven't found out all of the facts yet. Don't get me wrong, knowledge is crucial; however, without knowing how to use that knowledge, life becomes tedious and difficult to understand, because there are always other people involved in your life.

You can be the smartest person in the world, but without wisdom you cannot live successfully in this world. Why? Because life is all about relating to others. Real life involves the dynamic and always changing character of human behavior. It involves the emotions of people and the way they behave under certain conditions. The movie, *Beautiful Mind,* is a great example of a very smart man who could not relate to others.

All of us need wisdom to live life to its fullest. The thing that separates knowledge ("smartness") from wisdom is that wisdom is how you use knowledge. In my life, wisdom has become associated with relationships: a relationship with God and others. In the verse above, wisdom comes from God. What this means is that God has a purpose for your life that is defined by how you relate to others using His attributes. Wisdom comes from God when we begin to understand what He means when He says that He loves you unconditionally, when He forgives you, when He shows you grace in a situation, and so on.

Wisdom comes only from God, because only God knows your heart and everyone else's heart. God has given you the Holy Spirit to lead you to serve others in His name. When we live with the wisdom that comes from God, we see people as God sees them...hurting, lonely, confused, without direction, etc. Stretch yourself to become spiritually discerning about the way God sees you and others. This is the wisdom that God wants to give us generously.

His original purpose for man was a healthy relationship with Him and each other. Our "smartness" has removed God from living a life that involves others. We run roughshod over others because of what we call our "smartness." Begin today to ask God for wisdom. When He gives it to you, it will not be in the form of knowledge, but rather in the form of trust and obedience of who He is and what He has done for you. You will then be free to love others as God loves them, to forgive others as God has forgiven them, to sacrifice for them as God has sacrificed for you. Your life will be lived to its fullest with God's wisdom that will always include others.

32

GOD
CARES FOR YOU

Cast all your anxiety on him because he cares for you.

—1 PETER 5:7

I ADMIRE THOSE PEOPLE WHO don't seem to have a care in this world. I wonder if they are even human. I know that I have had anxiety in my life, and it doesn't feel good. We experience anxiety when the future is not clear and decisions have to be made. We experience anxiety when our thoughts dwell on ourselves and our physical condition. We experience anxiety over what others might do to the things we have. The common aspect to the sources of anxiety is the unknown. We do not like the unknown - it scares us.

What do we do to try to eliminate anxiety in our lives? First of all, I think we try to ignore it. This is useless because there will always be "stuff" to remind us of what we don't know will happen. Those that are mentally oriented will try to reason why they have anxiety. If they are successful, then they will come up with a list to follow, so that anxiety does not become part of their life. They had might as well try to raise the Titanic. It won't work.

Some people will try to get busy to forget about the thing that causes anxiety. This is probably the most prominent way that people use to remove anxiety. "If I can stay busy enough, I will not be thinking about the future unknowns that cause anxiety." We are only misleading ourselves into thinking that we can control our own anxieties.

Anxiety can eat up a person to the point that their physical and mental conditions are negatively impacted. One of my "tongue-in-cheek" remedies for anxiety is to go and buy some dark chocolate (most of you would settle for milk chocolate; I have to have dark chocolate). This does not get us anywhere other than more anxiety over the way we feel and look after eating all of that chocolate. Another example is when people set a goal for what they would call financial freedom. When they reach that goal, they have some other aspect of life bopping them on the head and causing more anxiety.

Now, read the verse above carefully. What's not in the verse? We all become anxious over something. So, what God does not say in the verse above is that He will remove it from you. I think that's what most of us would want God to do is to remove anxiety from our lives. But, we would be missing the most important aspect of our relationship with God: trust.

God says to cast your anxiety on Him, Jesus Christ. The question to every Believer is, "How do I cast my anxiety onto Christ?" First of all, you need to admit that you have anxiety about something. Anxiety is the tight feeling in your stomach accompanied by nervousness in your whole body. Anxiety can reach a point of totally paralyzing your life, because you are so deep into anxiety. Anxiety is there, because you are thinking of only yourself. You see, when God says to cast your anxiety onto Christ, He is actually saying "trust" Christ for the unknowns in your life.

Let me repeat this because it is the root of anxiety. Where do you put your trust in the things that are unknown? If you naturally live each day thinking that you are in control, and you can work everything out no matter how tough. Then you will discover all of the unknowns that cause anxiety and will find yourself totally out of control. You are trusting yourself for your future. That's scary! This is a big NO-NO for a Believer.

As a Believer, you have trusted your eternal life to Jesus Christ. Why can't you trust your worldly life to Him? The Bible states clearly that God has given you everything that you need to live a Godly life on this earth. He has made you a co-heir with Christ to the inheritance that Christ receives. He has declared that you are one of His children. He has said that He will protect you until you are with Him. Now, do you see that your anxiety is where you are trusting yourself and not trusting God?

Today, ask the Holy Spirit to reveal to you who you are trusting for your daily life on this earth. It will probably be "yourself." When you understand this, agree with God that you have not been trusting Him and you want to start today to walk in the Spirit with complete trust in God for your life. When you cast your anxiety on Christ, you will experience the full and abundant life that God desires for you.

33

YOUR LIFE
SPIRITUAL GIFT

Each one should use whatever gift he has received to serve others, faithfully administering God's grace in its various forms. If anyone speaks, he should do it as one speaking the very words of God. If anyone serves, he should do it with the strength God provides, so that in all things God may be praised through Jesus Christ. To him be the glory and the power for ever and ever. Amen.

—1 PETER 4:10-11

THESE ARE POWERFUL VERSES FOR every Believer. Every Believer has received a spiritual gift empowered by the Holy Spirit. If every member of the body exercises their spiritual gift, then the needs of the body are met. The particular gift that you have comes from God. He knows the needs of others and has equipped you to serve others in the very area that they need.

A Believer's spirituality is determined by the practical use of their gift. In other words, a Believer grows spiritually when they are serving others using their spiritual gift. Unfortunately, many Believers do not exercise their "spirituality" and the needs of others go unmet. If you don't know what your spiritual gift is, don't wait to find out before you start serving others. It is very likely that God will show you your spiritual gift as you are serving others.

Also, note that "grace" is a part of every one's spiritual gift. All of us need to be reminded of God's grace. Grace is getting something you don't deserve, and mercy is not getting what you do deserve. Try thinking of someone that rubs you the wrong way, and guess what God would want you to give that person: grace! Don't you know that you show God's grace given to you by the way you treat others? That's our big problem as Believers. We don't fully comprehend the grace that God has shown us. We all need to know God's grace for us more and more, deeper and deeper on a continuous basis. If our understanding of God's grace is faulty, there is no way we will be a living testimony to God's grace. Some people may even say, "If that is what God's grace looks like, then I don't want any of it!"

If you open your mouth make sure it is only what God would have you say. Can you imagine how much quieter the world would be if Believers only said things that were encouraging and uplifting to brothers and sisters in Christ? Their testimony for Jesus Christ would also be phenomenal. Believers have a tendency to say things that are in their hearts and minds. This is not necessarily bad except for the thoughts that may be going on inside of us. If there is a warning bell going off in you about your attitude, please do not say anything. You will probably not be using your spiritual gift at times like that.

Serving others should be unconditional...no strings attached. What we have a tendency to do is judge the person as to whether they really have a need. When you are exercising a spiritual gift, you don't ask if the person really deserves what you are doing for them. You also don't get upset if they don't thank you for helping them. You really don't get upset if they get upset for what you did for them. In all of these cases, it is God that is being shown to others through your life.

Also, there is the "endurance" perspective. Many of us, if not all of us, can put on a front and serve others with what looks like a Christ-like attitude only to become tired and weary of serving others. I know of a man whose wife was diagnosed with Alzheimer's disease. He quit his job and for the next 12 years personally took care of his wife. When he discussed how he could do it, his answer was only by the power of the Holy Spirit and God's grace shown to him through his wife's illness. Your power to serve others and to exercise a spiritual gift comes ONLY from the Holy Spirit. If you try to serve using only your flesh, you will grow tired, weary, stressful, angry, bitter, and, eventually, give up.

Read the verses again and look for the "why" you have a spiritual gift. Why? So that in all things God will be praised, so that Christ will be glorified.

Maybe we should ALWAYS be remembering the grace that God gives us even though we don't deserve it. Maybe we should empty ourselves of all of our fleshly motives for why we help others. Maybe we should become weak so that God can become strong in our lives. So, don't get all tied up in knots over your spiritual gift. God gave it to you so that He would be honored. Now, go and serve others so that God will be glorified!

34

YOUR LIFE
CORRECT OBEDIENCE

"The most important one," answered Jesus, "is this: 'Hear, O Israel, the Lord our God, the Lord is one. Love the Lord your God with all your heart and with all your soul and with all your mind and with all your strength.' The second is this: 'Love your neighbor as yourself.' There is no commandment greater than these."

—MARK 12:29-31

LIVING THE CHRISTIAN LIFE CAN be very difficult and confusing. I hear so many times how people want to become better Christians. It's usually phrased in what they are doing to become better. For example, "I'm reading the entire Bible in one year." "I've been attending church for the past year and have not missed a Sunday." "I have been on a mission trip this year and it was great!" "I pray for people every day." "I never go to church without my Bible." "I worked in Vacation Bible School this year." All of these sound great from a religious point of view. However, behind each one of these is a motive as to why the person did what they did. Are we trying to be obedient to the laws of man as opposed to having a heart for God and others?

In the verses above, Jesus was answering a question posed by one of the theologically educated people (a teacher of the Old Testament). He wanted to know the greatest commandment. I guess he wanted to make sure he was at least obedient to the most important law. Being the teacher that he was, you would suspect that he knew the answer. His motive may have been to look good to others that were standing around with Jesus. Or, it may have been to trap Jesus (this happened frequently when Jesus was with the so-called theological giants of the time). Or, he may have been genuinely interested in the answer. When you ask questions today in classes or with other people, which of these motives is prompting you to ask your questions? The first two motives are extremely "self" driven with no pure and sincere interest in getting to the truth. The last motive should be our reason to ask questions: because we are genuinely interested in the answer.

What's more interesting is the man's response to the answer that Jesus gave him. He agreed with Jesus and added that to love God and serve others was more important than rituals that appear to be religious. This was dangerous ground for the man, but he saw the truth and stated it as the truth. Jesus then told him that he had answered wisely and that he was not far from the Kingdom of God. The man's obedience had the correct motive.

So, what must you do to be a better Christian? The first thing is not to think of YOU! This means to not think about what you should be doing that is the acceptable customs or rituals for Christians today. Going to church (wearing certain clothes to church), reading your Bible, going on a mission trip, and even praying can be a very selfish activity. Instead of trying to figure out how you can become a better Christian, God says to love Him and to love others.

THAT LEAVES THE "YOU" IN YOU OUT! The "you" in you will be taken care of by God through the Holy Spirit. He has given you all of the spiritual blessings to live a godly life here on earth. You don't need to continually evaluate yourself as to how you are doing as a Christian. I know this may be hurting your brain…it did mine until I read the verses above and realized that I was no longer living by the law but living with the grace that God has shown me through His Son, Jesus Christ.

It is with this attitude of grace that God wants and expects me to interact with others. God's grace motivates me to correct obedience, because I am focused on God and others and not on myself. By doing so, others will not be looking at my level of spiritual maturity or lack of it. Instead, they will be praising and glorifying the Lord God Almighty.

35

THE BIBLE
A BOOK TO READ

Now the Bereans were of more noble character than the
Thessalonians, for they received the message with great
eagerness and examined the Scriptures every day to see if
what Paul said was true.

—ACTS 17:11

THE BIBLE IS BY FAR a best seller. Many homes have more than one
Bible. Bibles are given at births, dedications, graduations, marriages,
and other significant life events. Most hotel rooms have a Bible in the
nightstand drawer. There are numerous translations of the Bible, and
it continues to be translated into every language known to man. You
probably have your own Bible or your family has a Bible. The question is
always asked, "How often do you read your Bible?"

In the verse above, there were Jews from the city of Berea who heard
Paul preach in their synagogue. The Bereans had a reputation of being
more "noble" than people in other cities in the area. Referring to someone
as "noble" meant that they lived their lives with higher standards as seen
through their character.

These Bereans appear to have been very interested in what Paul talked
about. Even though it is not stated in the verse, Paul talked about Jesus
Christ and forgiveness of sins through His sacrifice on the cross. Paul
also told them about the love and grace of God as seen through Jesus

Christ. He probably described the resurrection of Christ as his hope in a future eternity with God. The Bereans became extremely interested in everything that Paul said to the point that they went to the Scriptures they had, and began to search for proof of what Paul had said.

Now, the Scriptures ("Bible") that the Bereans had were most likely the books of the Old Testament. It is possible that they may have had copies of letters that Paul wrote to Thessalonica. 1 & 2 Thessalonians were among the first letters that Paul wrote, and Thessalonica was close by (only 50 miles from Berea). However, even if they had only the Old Testament (called the "Tanakh" by the Jews at that time), they would have found many prophecies of the coming of Christ. As a matter of fact, until Paul started writing his letters that are included in what we call the New Testament, the only Scriptures available between the time of Christ and Paul's letters was the Old Testament. In other words, people became Christians during the early church by people telling them about Jesus Christ. The gospel was all verbal testimony using the prophecies contained in the Old Testament. We could learn some lessons from the early church by becoming more verbal about our testimony for Christ.

What makes the Bereans stand out is their eagerness to examine their Bible to find the truth. Today, we are woefully ignorant of God's Word. As common, everyday Christians, we have relegated the study of Scripture to Pastors and theologians. It is too easy a cop-out to rely on someone else to interpret Scripture for us.

We use all kinds of excuses. "Since there are so many translations, who knows which one is accurate?" It is highly likely that the Bereans were using a Greek translation of the Old Testament. They did not let translations stand in their way to study the Scriptures. Another excuse is that it is difficult to understand. Well, within God's Word it says that no one can understand the Bible except by the Holy Spirit. I'm afraid that a lot of us try to understand the Bible with our own minds and intellect. We do this because we can then interpret the Bible the way we want to. It is only the Holy Spirit that can reveal truths from the Bible. We must learn to study the Bible relying on the Holy Spirit and not on our own understanding.

I was 30 years old when the Bible became a "must" for me to read. I had been a Christian for 18 years and had read the Bible for what I could get out of it...my own understanding. Guess what? I did not understand it! I had even taught Bible classes. But I used my own intellect and not the Holy Spirit. After I got rid of the "me" in reading the Bible, God began to show me His truths in His Word. I felt like scales fell from my eyes, that the veil over my brain had been lifted, and that there was no longer a law for me to read His Word. I eagerly devoured the Bible on a daily basis.

My best suggestion for a Believer to get into the Bible is to stop looking at what you can get out of it, and start learning about God from His Word. Read what He says about Himself. The Holy Spirit will reveal God to you. The scales will fall and the veil will disappear. Your life will never be the same.

36

YOUR LIFE
WHAT TO DO WHEN
TIMES ARE TOUGH

> If calamity comes upon us, whether the sword of judgment,
> or plague or famine, we will stand in your presence before
> this temple that bears your Name and will cry out to you
> in our distress, and you will hear us and save us.
>
> —2 CHRONICLES 20:9

THIS VERSE OFFERS HOPE FOR every tough situation that you can find yourself experiencing. This verse is in the middle of a calamity for the Hebrew people living in and around Jerusalem. There was a massive army marching toward them that looked like it could wipe them off the face of the earth. Talk about a calamity!

There is an undercurrent of "calamity" going on in the world today. Sometimes we all feel like everything is out of control. These calamities are so big that they look like the end of the world is just around the corner. Examples of these calamities are the ongoing work to resolve the oil spills, the future of health care in the U.S., and, the impact of natural disasters (hurricanes, tornados, tsunamis, etc.). As soon as the world gets through one calamity, another one comes along. It reminds me of when I was a child swimming in the ocean. Wave after wave kept breaking on the shore. Some of those waves were huge and would knock me down and it would hurt.

Many of us in the United States appreciate that we live in a very unique country in the history of man. When times are good, we say that God has blessed us. However, when times get tough and calamity occurs, we want to get back to the good times as quickly as possible. We all yearn for that "happy place" where life is good and easy. All of us would have to admit that we are "spoiled." We really want everything to be OK with us every minute of our lives.

With this "spoiled" attitude, we look on all calamities as bad for us. What is interesting about the verse above is the underlying principle of one of the causes for calamity. Reread the verse and you can see the words "sword of judgment." God judges. He has to judge. We would not want to live in a world where God does not judge. However, in the verse above the word "us" is used meaning the children of God. As Believers, that's you and me! In other words, some of the bad times are from God as judgment. Now, compare that with our "spoiled" attitude and the result is a life lived apart from God - a life of fear, uncertainty, and despair.

The speaker of the verse above is King Jehoshaphat. I have always loved to say his name. He is praying to God about their situation. Notice that Jehoshaphat says that no matter what the calamity is, he and his people will acknowledge God for who He is. Jehoshaphat also says that they will turn to God and seek His help. There are too many people who want someone other than God to help them these days. In our spoiled situation in the U.S., we always turn to the government to resolve our calamities. King Jehoshaphat was the government! He realized that the calamity that they were facing was beyond human solutions. God answered Jehoshaphat's prayer by sending the Holy Spirit. Everything worked out to the good.

How should a Believer react to calamities? How do you react to calamities? Consider the following for the calamities in your life.

(1) **There is a God and He is always in control.** He created everything, and He will bring everything to an end.

(2) **God knows what you are going through and knows how much you can take.** All of the calamities that Job went through were with God's OK. When Jesus was facing the cross, He knew that the pain and torture that He would be experiencing was a necessary part of God's plan for providing salvation for us.

(3) **Instead of spending time on the "why is this happening to me" question, look for ways to help others through the calamity.** After all, Jesus said that all of the commands of God

are wrapped up in, "Love your God with all your strength, mind, and heart and love others as yourself."

(4) **Everything that happens can end in glory to God.** This is a tough one, but if you think about the eternal versus the temporary, your trust and faith in God will grow. He knows what He is doing.

Back to my personal example of riding the waves: it hurt sometimes when I got knocked down by the big waves. But I liked the big waves; they were fun. So, I'd go right back into the ocean to wait on the next big wave. I would have missed the exhilaration of riding out a big wave if I had given up and just sat on the beach watching the waves. It sure was fun to experience the waves. Consider it pure joy when you face many trials. (James 1:2)

37

YOUR LIFE
WHAT ARE YOU AFRAID OF?

The LORD is my light and my salvation—whom shall I fear? The LORD is the stronghold of my life—of whom shall I be afraid?

—PSALM 27:1

I LOVE THE VERSE ABOVE. It contains the answer to everything that the world has thrown at me to fear. Before I talk about those things, you must realize what fear does to a person. Fear is paralyzing. Just like a "deer in the headlights," we lose all mobility and ability to think when fear strikes us. Being afraid changes our personality. We can become overly concerned and worried because of fear, to the point of not being aware of what is going on around us with those we love. Being afraid is basically letting our mind start to envision the "what ifs" and the "perceptions of what might be."

For example, a basic fear for a whole lot of people is when someone else is driving a vehicle while they are the passenger. Our mind begins to go through the dangers of how fast they are driving or how close they follow the car in front of them or how they keep looking at you and not the road. You want to scream, "Keep your eyes on the road!" Talk about a fear of what might happen! We breathe a silent prayer when we safely arrive at our destination. As a matter of fact, every fear that we face originates with what goes on in this world: fear for the future of America, fear for our children and grandchildren, fear of a job loss, fear of the loss of a loved one. So, fear is a worldly thing! It is not a spiritual thing! I know many of you reading this will disagree with me. But, remember another verse from God's Word that basically says that where there is perfect love (God), there is no fear. (Philippians 2:12)

Now, reread the verse above. The "light" that reveals the truth about everything was created by God. He is the author and originator of light that penetrates any and every darkness (or fear) for you to be able to see the truth. For example, when you experience a fear for America, the spiritual light from God reveals the truth that all of the nations of the earth and their governments are determined and set in place by God (read Romans 13). You can either believe that people have the ultimate authority or that God is in control. You get to decide. If you choose to believe authority resides in people, you will constantly be in fear (just like when someone else is driving the vehicle you are riding in). With every fear you experience, ask the Holy Spirit to show you the truth through the revealing light of God about the circumstances of that fear. You will find that you have been putting your trust in people and not God.

The verse also says that the LORD is your salvation. The light that reveals our salvation reveals the death, burial, and resurrection of Jesus Christ. When you believe that you have something to do with your salvation, you are subject to how you "feel" or how you "don't feel" saved. It is God who provides your salvation. With God's light and with His salvation why should you be afraid?

The last part of the verse is HUGE for every Believer. To live the life of a Believer in this world, you must trust God just like you trust Him for your salvation. He must be your "stronghold." A "stronghold" is a fortress used for safety, security, refuge, and survival. It is interesting that everyone develops "strongholds" in their life to protect their attitudes and feelings. This is done over time one brick at a time.

If God is not your stronghold, then you will develop ways of insulating yourself from others because you don't want to get hurt again. For example, a negative stronghold is avoidance of people, places, or events that have caused us pain. The problem with this kind of stronghold is that it implants fear in our lives to the point of enslaving us to certain personal behaviors. We cannot be a person who is loving God and serving others. Don't get me wrong. As Believers, we can truly love God and others, but when our "self" is endangered, we revert back to our personal worldly strongholds. Again, you either trust your "self" or you put your trust in God.

Everyone, including Believers, will experience fear in their lives. When fear first hits us, as Believers, we need to ask ourselves the question, "Will I trust people (including yourself) or will I trust God?" This is the decision that all of us have to make almost every day of our lives. The more fear you experience is an indicator that you are probably trusting people more than God. The more you answer, "I will trust God!" the more God becomes a stronghold for your life. When God is your stronghold, your life will be one of joy, peace, patience, kindness, goodness, faithfulness, gentleness and self-control. (Galatians 5:22) And then you will experience the "peace that cannot be understood." Your life will be a testimony to God's glory.

38

HOLY SPIRIT
BRINGS GLORY TO CHRIST

He will bring glory to me by taking from what is mine
and making it known to you.

—JOHN 16:14

THIS IS WHAT JESUS WAS telling His disciples on the night He was
betrayed and, the next day, crucified. Jesus had been trying to calm
their fears by telling them what will happen to Him. In this verse, "He"
is the Holy Spirit. In John chapters 14-16, Jesus had been describing the
role of the Holy Spirit in the life of a Believer. Jesus said that He must go
so that the "Counselor" (Holy Spirit) would come. Why? Because the
power of God is the Holy Spirit and Jesus wanted that power to reside in
Believers.

Every Believer has the Holy Spirit living within them. The power that
created all of creation dwells within a Believer. The power that raised Jesus
from the dead lives in a Believer. The power that healed the sick and made
the lame to walk is within a Believer. This is awesome spiritual power. It
is the Holy Spirit.

It is the talking of "power" of the Holy Spirit that makes some people
nervous. Yet, Jesus gave us the Holy Spirit so that we would know God
better. This includes spiritual things. When I read about the Holy Spirit
in the New Testament, I always come away with the understanding that I
know nothing spiritually apart from the Holy Spirit. Any spiritual changes

in my heart or mind or soul are a result of the power of the Holy Spirit. No one (not Billy Graham, not a Pastor, not the most intellectual theologian, not me and not you) can learn anything spiritual except by the Holy Spirit. I think this is one of the biggest weaknesses for Believers today. We try to do things ourselves.

Jesus knew that His followers could choose to live a life that would be "self" focused rather than "God" focused. Jesus knew we needed help. So, He decided to give every Believer the Holy Spirit to empower them to live a Godly life. Why? So that He, Jesus, would be identified, honored, and glorified through the life of a Believer.

When we live a life that is selfish, any identification, honor, or glorification given by others is expected to be for us. We expect people to think more highly of us. "Look at me!" "Look what I did!" The truth is that most people are not thinking about YOU! They are too busy thinking about themselves (selfish living), just like you! It's sort of like the whole world is thinking only of themselves with little or no thought of others.

I heard an expression of how to describe people who are totally about themselves, and I think it is very descriptive. People who are consumed with themselves are "staring at their navels." They become an expert of their own navel because they want to think only about themselves. There is probably nothing sadder than when God sees His children caught up in "navel staring." They have their heads down and can't see those who are in need around them. They can't see God at work in the world. They have no power to do anything except to bump into something because they are "staring at their navels."

Jesus gave Believers the Holy Spirit so that we would have all the power necessary to live a Godly life on earth. We are complete with the Holy Spirit. The Holy Spirit shares with us the spiritual knowledge of God and Christ so that we understand things from a spiritual perspective. This allows us to see others around us and to see God at work. We experience the power of the Holy Spirit when things happen and we know it wasn't because of us. It is at these moments that we glorify Christ and others glorify Him.

A Believer's life becomes a living testimony for Christ (rather than themselves) when the Believer is relying on the Holy Spirit. As Believers, we lack nothing. We can truly allow the Holy Spirit to lead us and guide us into those things that will bring glory and honor to Christ. The results of such a life are joy, peace, and patience. How are you living your life? Staring at your navel or allowing the Holy Spirit to lead and guide you? It's your choice on a daily basis.

39

GOD
ALWAYS DOES WHAT
IS BEST FOR YOU

So the LORD scattered them from there over all the earth, and they stopped building the city. That is why it was called Babel —because there the LORD confused the language of the whole world. From there the LORD scattered them over the face of the whole earth.

—GENESIS 11:8-9

GOD ALWAYS DOES WHAT IS best for you in your relationship with Him even when it looks like things could not get any worse. The verses above come long after the devastation resulting from the Flood that covered the earth. From Noah's family, the world was repopulated. Generations came and went. People heard stories about the Great Flood. They heard about God. In the meantime, Nimrod became a great leader of the people. Cities were built. People were busy living their lives. They became independent. They didn't need God. They began to build structures for themselves. They wanted to do things that would bring glory to them. They wanted to gaze upon what they had done and say, "Look what we did!"

Does that sound like us today? Nothing has changed. We all want to do something so we can say, "Look what I did!" We are driven by the flesh to take pride in our own flesh. The life of every Believer is to be lived completely for the glory of God. I am afraid that most Believers are living for themselves. We have been deceived by the things of this world. These things become our idols and consume large gobs of our time.

It is at these times, thankfully, that God intervenes in our lives to get our attention. He did this to the people referenced in the verses above. He actually made life more difficult for them, which does not sound too good. But, His objective was to bring them back to Him. God removed the things of this world that enabled them to seek their own glory. It is interesting that the city that they were building was called "Babel" because God prohibited them from being able to communicate with one another. Their common language used to communicate no longer existed. They were talking to each other but they could not understand what was being said. Today, if someone is speaking but we don't understand, we say they are "babbling."

I thank God for doing the same thing in my life. When a Believer begins to forget God and take credit for God's work done in that Believer's life, God will intervene to bring that Believer back to Him. Oh, we fuss and fidget over God's way of getting us back to Him, but I believe He knows exactly what it will take to get us back. Although His way usually involves a tougher life on earth for us, I don't think God is penalizing us. He just loves us so much that He'll do anything (even when we don't like what He does) to keep us close to Him.

One of these days, you and I will understand completely why God does what He does. We will not disagree or even complain, but will bow before Him and tell Him that all of His work in our lives was exactly what we needed. The next time you think your life has gotten harder, consider your relationship to God. Have you been thinking of Him? Have you been trusting God for everything about your life? Have you given Him the glory whenever the Spirit has prompted you? Have you been diligently studying His Word – the Bible? Are your prayers directed toward His kingdom to come and that His will be done?

God earnestly desires a relationship with you that is closer than any relationship on this earth (including marriage). What are you doing to maintain a healthy relationship with God? Do you trust Him with everything in your life even when it looks like life gets harder? God knows what He is doing, and He is doing things that are best for you.

40

YOUR LIFE
GROWING CHRIST-LIKE

Being confident of this, that he who began a good work
in you will carry it on to completion until the day of
Christ Jesus.

—PHILIPPIANS 1:6

THIS IS MY PERSONAL FAVORITE verse from the Bible. When I meditate
on this verse, I receive a positive, healthy, hopeful, and complete
perspective of God's work in my life.

The verse begins with a statement of confidence. Paul, who wrote the
book of Philippians, describes his attitude as being confident. You know
you just can't say you are confident about something unless you have grown
to trust something. For me, the confidence I have now, when it comes
to God working in my life, is a result of trials and errors, good times and
bad times, and doing the right things and the wrong things. Through all
of these interactions with God (bad and good), I came to realize that, as a
Believer, when I obey Him, He is pleased. When I disobey Him, He will
discipline me (for my own good), but He will always love me and love me
unconditionally. As a Believer, if you spend time thinking on the fact that
God loves you just as you are, your confidence in God will increase.

Now, what does the verse say that you should have confidence in?
And, this is what's so exciting about this verse. The confidence is that
God started a work in you when you became a Believer and He continues

this work every day of your life. This "good work" is to mold and shape your life to be Christ-like. I don't know about you, but when I realized that God was doing this work, I had the thought that He sure was going to have to work hard.

This work occurs through getting to know God and His Word. Many people tell me about the hunger they have for God's Word. Well, given our own human inclination, human beings would rather be satisfying the needs of the flesh (e.g., watching TV). When you as a Believer see the value of God's Word in your life, the Holy Spirit will put zeal in your heart, soul, and mind so that you can't wait to read and study God's Word. You want to know more about God. This is part of the "work" that God does in your life.

God also uses relationships with others. This work of His is huge in our lives. You see, I don't believe in coincidences, luck, or fate in a Believer's life. Believers are the children of God! He cares for everything that happens to you and what you go through in this world. He knows the number of hairs on your head (that's easy for Him in my case).

From God's perspective, you have accepted His Son Jesus Christ as your Lord and Savior. God thinks that this is the ultimate in having a relationship with Him because this is what He planned before He created anything. You are unbelievably important to God. You are in His hands at all times. He sees and knows everything that you do. This is the reason that He starts this work in you. He knows the best life for you to live on this earth is one that is lived with Christ-likeness as opposed to self-likeness.

Another aspect of God's work in our lives is that we can't do it ourselves. I cannot change myself into Christ-likeness. Only God can do this! He is doing it and will continue to do that work every hour of every day. I also like that there are no conditions for His work. If I'm asleep, He's at work. If I'm at work, He's at work. If I'm eating, playing, watching TV, or whatever, He's at work. I love that thought...God is always at work in my life.

There comes a time when God will stop His work in your life according to the verse above. He stops working when you either go to be with Christ (you die physically) or when Christ returns. The point is that God keeps working until you are with Him. Just writing this has me on Cloud Nine or should I say has me thinking of heaven. Know that, as a Believer, God is ALWAYS at work in you. He never takes a holiday or a vacation. He never gives up on you because of your actions. He never gets tired and takes a nap. He never, ever forgets about you. You are always the center of His attention as one of His children. It does not get any better than that!

41

YOUR THOUGHTS
PAY ATTENTION TO WHAT
YOU ARE THINKING

> Now this is what the LORD Almighty says: "Give careful thought to your ways. You have planted much, but have harvested little. You eat, but never have enough. You drink, but never have your fill. You put on clothes, but are not warm. You earn wages, only to put them in a purse with holes in it." This is what the LORD Almighty says: "Give careful thought to your ways."
>
> —HAGGAI 1:5-7

THESE ARE FANTASTIC VERSES TO consider what it means to think "spiritually" contrasted with what it means to think "worldly." God tells us to "Give careful thought to your ways."

Most of us do a lot of thinking when we go about doing things. A lot of these thoughts are not necessarily healthy. There is not much we do as human beings that is not preceded by what we think about something before we do that something. I don't know if that sentence makes sense, but I think it does. What I'm trying to say is that if someone asks us to do something there is a hesitation before we tell the person that we will do what they ask. Now, there can be all kinds of thoughts going through a person's head when this happens. Thoughts like, "Why don't they do it themselves?" or, "Why are you asking me?" or, "Do I have time to do this?" or, "Why don't you ask someone else?"

The thoughts we have before we take action come from the way we look at the world. And, the way we look at the world comes from pieces in all of our past experiences. I think all of you would agree that from the world's perspective, a person would be all about themselves. This world view would have a set of values that originate and end with each person. Each person decides what is good/bad, healthy/unhealthy, beneficial/unprofitable, and, especially, what is right/wrong. The verses above describe a person who has this kind of selfish world view. The ultimate end of a selfish life lived only for that person is emptiness. That person may have a lot of things during their life but all of their accumulated things do not satisfy the real, genuine, and true need of human beings: relationships built on unconditional love.

The verses above say that "you planted much, but harvested little." This is like working for a company with the goal of earning a lot of money, so that you won't have financial problems. There are too many life testimonies of people who have placed their priority on their job for their whole life and end up with that company saying, "You've been one of the hardest working employees we've ever had, but now we don't need you." You planted a lot but end up with nothing. Your goal should have been to prioritize your spouse and family. You can have that goal and still give your best to a company. The problem is not who you worked for; it's what you set as your personal goal: to make money.

This same "world view" is seen in the other parts of the verses above. An unrealistic value placed on food, drink, and clothes can set you up for a world view of selfishness. I know you may be wondering about food and drink but unless, as a Believer, you think that God provides all that you need, you will build a structure of belief in your life that says, "Look what I've got!" It is so much easier to become a part of this kind of world view, because that's all we see on TV, in movies, in our neighbors and, even in our families. Clothes have become ridiculous. The price we pay for someone to wash jeans until they are faded and then tear holes in them is about as far away as you can get from God calling you a good steward of the resources He has given you. We need to give careful thought to our ways!

Finally, the ending of the verses above include what we do with money. There is nothing wrong with money from the Bible's point of view. God has provided for everyone who belongs to Him. Where Christians get into trouble with money is when we see it as a way to buy our happiness or to hoard the money for our own future use (which is usually squandered by our children or grandchildren, or even our government). As Believers, we also use money to purchase our social standing, so that others can see that we have the same or more than they do; in other words, "Look at my success."

All of this is a "rat race" to look better than the next person. The problem is that everyone else may have the same philosophy of living; so, the measure of success escalates and escalates...you'll never reach that goal! What a waste of God's resources! You will agree when I say that it looks like the more money someone makes, the more holes they find in their pockets and the more money they must make. This never ends when your goal for earning money is set on the things of this world. God says to "give careful thought to your ways!"

God is asking you in these verses to consider seriously what your thoughts are on living life on this earth. Is it all about you? Or, is it all about living a life for Him? Most of you are now thinking of ways to justify or rationalize what you have. Don't! If your use of God's resources has been wasted on you, ask God to forgive you, know that He has forgiven you, and start giving careful thoughts to your life. Your life goal should be to bring glory to God! You can't do that when you are juggling all the things in this world that would seem to provide a happy life. The world is not here to provide you a happy life. It is here to take from you everything that will satisfy the deepest needs in your life. God has provided everything you need to have all of those deepest needs met by loving Him and serving others.

42

CHURCH

YOUR PREPARATION TO ATTEND

Guard your steps when you go to the house of God. Go near to listen rather than to offer the sacrifice of fools, who do not know that they do wrong. Do not be quick with your mouth, do not be hasty in your heart to utter anything before God. God is in heaven and you are on earth, so let your words be few.

—ECCLESIASTES 5:1-2

I AM POSITIVE THAT MANY of you are wondering, "Where in the world did these verses come from?" They come from the book written by the wisest man who has ever lived, King Solomon. Ecclesiastes contains the results of an "experiment" that Solomon performed on himself. He had the resources to live life any way he chose, so he decided to try different things to see what could make "man" happy. He tried wealth, possessions, honor, work, sex, food, etc. and nothing made him happy. Solomon would violently disagree with the beer commercial that says, "It doesn't get any better than this!" The book uses the word "meaningless" about 50 times to describe how everything on this earth ends in "meaninglessness." The book ends with the conclusion to "fear God and keep His commandments." The verses above come near the middle of the book. Solomon pauses in describing his various experiments to describe a person's attitude in going to the "house of God" or what we call going to "church" today.

The verses say to guard your steps. Steps indicate a direction and a movement in that direction. This "guarding" involves your attitude in preparing to worship God. For me, and for probably a lot of you, it's very easy to be thinking about a lot of other things when you get ready to go to church or on your way to church. You could be thinking about your job, or an incident with your spouse or children, or something that has been bugging you over the past few weeks. May I say that this is worldly thinking. It will be impossible to hear from God, if your thoughts are tied up with yourself. You must prepare yourself to hear from God.

The verses go on to say that we should prepare ourselves to listen. It is interesting that the verses say that listening is God's choice for our worship of Him instead of sacrifices. This makes sense, because frequently we treat church attendance as another check off on our list of what we think it means to be a good Christian. But we miss God! It is imperative to hear from God first and then take action on what He reveals to us. Too often, we have already made up our minds what "church" will be like and we bring those expectations to church with us. This is all about ourselves and what we think we should be getting out of church. God has something entirely different in mind.

Look at the other things in these verses that God says to be careful with...your mouth and your heart. Your mouth will express what has accumulated in your heart all week. I hope you realize how spiritually dangerous this is. When we open our mouths to express our thoughts without first seeking God's guidance, nothing but trouble can result. This is why there are so many hurt feelings when people visit a church. Instead of speaking spiritual truths with others, we want to talk about the latest on politics, sports figures, or community news that has nothing to do with the worship of God. Some people actually save up all of their stories so that they can share them at church. People who are visiting may truly be looking for a place that puts God first and not the world. All they hear are the same things they hear at work or in their neighborhood. Our mouths should be expressing our praise and thankfulness for God. That is worship.

The verses conclude describing the frame of mind that we all should have about our approach to the worship of God. He is in heaven, which is spiritual and eternal. We are on earth, which is worldly and temporal. In other words, our thoughts are worthless when compared to the spiritual revelation that God desires to give each of us through His Holy Spirit. It's as if we accept the garbage of this world as the truth, and God's revelation never comes into our minds. As Believers, may we all approach God with an expectation that He will show us where we are as human beings and where He wants us as Christ-like witnesses for Him.

43

YOUR LIFE
WHO IS IN CONTROL?

> You, however, are controlled not by the sinful nature
> but by the Spirit, if the Spirit of God lives in you. And
> if anyone does not have the Spirit of Christ, He does not
> belong to Christ.
>
> —ROMANS 8:9

I THOUGHT ONE OF THE critical marks of success was to have total control over my life. You know what I'm talking about? I would not be in debt so that money would not control my income. I would stay healthy so that sickness would not determine how I felt. My children would do exactly what I asked them to do without repeating myself a thousand times. I would not be tied down transporting my kids to every kind of practice and game ever invented. The yard would remain immaculate without mowing, fertilizing, etc. All of the electrical and mechanical equipment in my home would always function without my intervention. My car would always be in top running condition with no weird noises coming from the engine. And more! If all of these things were true, then I might have the time and energy to control my life. But, these things are not true, have never been true, and never will be true. Then, who am I fooling about who has control of my life? Me!

At one time, I loved doing some of the things listed above. It was my way of achieving some kind of success in this world. When I had finished working in the yard, I would step back, take a good look at it, and think to myself, "This looks good!" Now, there is nothing inherently wrong with this picture except for when I told my kids, "I am too busy to play with you; I have to cut the grass." Or, I told my wife that I was too busy to help her with something in the house. You see, I could have thought that I was in control of my life doing what I wanted to do. NO! I was controlled by the yard to the point that it was a higher priority than my relationship with my family. Oh, I wanted to cut the grass and get the satisfaction of seeing a well-groomed yard, but this is all about my sinful nature. The things of this world were appealing to my sinful nature that ultimately controls me (even though I thought I was in control).

The sinful nature is what all of us have when we are born. It is the source of our selfishness…wanting to do things our way. The problem is that you, as a creation of God, were never intended to be controlled by the sinful nature. God knew that a life controlled by the sinful nature was one of misery, doubt, boredom, and confusion. The sinful nature actually tells us a lie over and over: "You are ok; you can do anything you want; you are here to get things that make you happy; etc." I believed that lie and went about doing all kinds of things and thinking that I was in control. One day I realized the lie I was living: I was being controlled by the things of this earth. This is the greatest deception that Believers experience. Instead of living a life totally for God, we believe the sinful nature and live a life controlled by other things EVEN THOUGH WE THINK WE ARE IN CONTROL! How deceived we are!

The life lived in the Holy Spirit is entirely different. To live this life you must give up your own life. You must be willing to sacrifice all of the worldly stuff that you think gives you self esteem, value, pleasure, and control. God has made you a new creation resulting in peace, truth, love, joy, patience, meaning, value, and everything else you need to live an abundant and full life. The Spirit of Christ is the Holy Spirit revealing to you the mind of Christ so that you, as a Believer, will have the same attitude as Jesus. Jesus Christ has shown you how to live a life for God.

Jesus did only what God the Father told Him to do. That's called obedience and that's what being controlled by the Spirit is all about. You have a choice to be controlled by the sinful nature and end up with a lousy life, or to be controlled by the Holy Spirit and experience a life that you never thought possible. Which one do you choose?

44

GRACE
WHAT IT DOES FOR US

For the grace of God that brings salvation has appeared
to all men. It teaches us to say "No" to ungodliness and
worldly passions, and to live self-controlled, upright and
godly lives in this present age, while we wait for the
blessed hope—the glorious appearing of our great God and
Savior, Jesus Christ, who gave himself for us to redeem us
from all wickedness and to purify for himself a people that
are his very own, eager to do what is good.

—TITUS 2:11-14

THERE WAS NO WAY THAT I could reduce the number of verses from
the passage above. All of these words are needed for each of us to be
reminded of what the grace of God does for us.

The first part of the verses above makes it clear that God has revealed
His grace to everyone. If you ever wondered about some Eskimo or some
unknown group of people in Tibet, this says that God's grace that brings
salvation has been shown to them. You may be asking, "How?" Well,
frankly, I don't know how God does it. I do know that God revealed Himself
to me before I had any thought of Him. Don't restrict God to only your
perspective. He is powerful enough to reveal Himself to people in ways that
you and I would not understand. But, we can rest assured that He has shown
His grace to everyone in a way that is meaningful to each person.

I do not think that any of us understands God's grace completely. That's what makes His grace so exciting! As we continue to experience the transforming power of the Holy Spirit, our understanding of grace increases. When we contemplate His grace toward us, we want to say, "No!" to everything that corrupts our lives in this world. We become motivated by the grace that He gave us to live godly lives in the world. It's not that we "have" to obey; with God's grace in view, we "want" to obey Him. This motivation results in our desire to please Him.

The motivation to live a godly life increases when we consider the second coming of Christ. All Believers should be in a constant state of awareness that Jesus Christ could return at any moment to start in motion the "end times." I don't know if you have felt the excitement to realize that Jesus could return while you are reading this. All of our earthly possessions take on a much reduced significance when we think about our Blessed Hope – the appearing of Jesus Christ. Those Believers who are heavenly minded will not have their minds set on worldly things. Those Believers who are earthly minded cannot be doing the will of God. All Believers should be heavenly minded because Christ will return at any moment.

But there's more! Jesus gave Himself for you and me. He died on the cross for our sins. His blood was put on the more perfect altar in heaven so that all of our sins (past, present, and future) would be forgiven and forgotten. This is getting better and better! It is through Christ and the power of the Holy Spirit that you and I become more Christ-like in our attitudes and behavior. We have been redeemed from all wickedness. We have become a people that are His. I like the way the verses above put it, "...a people that are His very own." WOW! Just think that you and I are identified as belonging to Jesus Christ. You are His.

Because of His grace, of our having the power to live godly lives, and of our waiting on His return, we are eager to do good works. Our motivation to love God and to serve others hits an all time high when we think on His grace and His coming. We are able to do the works of Christ because we understand the results: others will glorify our God. These verses are amazing in the power that they can give to Believers to do good works. Do you wonder why there are not more Christians who can't wait to serve others? Let's not get all tied up in knots about how we think we could become better Christians, when God clearly gives us all the reasons for why we should live a life totally relying on Him.

With these thoughts from God's Word, every Believer should realize that God expects them to be eager to do good works. Good works are those activities, attitudes, and the spoken word that honors God and encourages others. Are you about doing good works? Or, do you think your life is so complicated and hard that you don't have time for God or others? God has given you all the grace that you need to do good works. Do you live like you believe that He has done that?

45

YOUR LIFE
ARE YOU FIRST OR LAST?

> Sitting down, Jesus called the Twelve and said, "If anyone wants to be first, he must be the very last, and the servant of all."
>
> —MARK 9:35

MANY OF YOU HAVE BEEN through a life situation where the oldest of the children had reached a point in their life where it was time to move out and be on their own. What is interesting is that, if there are any brothers or sisters, they immediately declare that what belonged to the one moving out is now theirs. "I get their room!" "I want the furniture!" There are not many thoughts about the one moving out...it is more about what they can gain.

A similar situation frequently occurs in a business environment. When a person vacates their office space, those around that space would "scavenge" that person's space to get what they wanted. Again, not many people think about the person leaving.

A final example of this same phenomenon is the way loved ones fight over the possessions of someone who has recently died. "I know he/she wanted me to have this." "This was intended for me." "That picture is mine!" "Those grass clippers are mine!" This example brings home the selfishness that is in all of us when our thoughts are on ourselves and not on others. I caution you that you may want to stop reading this Life-Changing Verse now. Read at your own risk.

All of these examples are similar to a situation described by the above verse. What Jesus said in this verse was prompted by a discussion that the disciples of Jesus had among themselves. What is most interesting about the disciples' discussion was that Jesus had just said that He was going to be betrayed and killed, and that He would rise again after three days. Now, if you had heard Jesus say that, you would think that your thoughts would be about what was to happen to Jesus. Not the disciples.

Instead of thinking about Christ, they started arguing about who was going to be the greatest! This was the second time that Jesus had told them about His death and His resurrection. Since the first time they heard it, I guess they had time to think about how His death would impact them. Does this sound like us?! Please agree, because it is just like us under similar circumstances (see examples above). We are all tempted to think about what we can get out of other people including those closest to us.

Jesus asked them what they were arguing about but none of them would answer. I think they felt embarrassment and guilt. But Jesus did not let it go. What He told them is in the verse above. His statement turns the philosophy of this world upside down and inside out. His statement should turn us upside down and inside out.

Wanting to be first in this world includes all of the examples above. You want something without any regard for others. You have this idea that you deserve what you want, and you don't care about others. I know some of you are rationalizing about past events in your life where this applies. I have!

But the TRUTH statement made by Jesus is so clear that it cannot be rationalized away. If you want to be first, you must become the very last. You must become a servant to everyone. Here comes the rationalization again! "God never intended for Christians to be a door mat!" Stop rationalizing your selfish desire to get what you want. Jesus, your Lord and Savior, was God in the flesh and He served everyone. He washed the feet of the disciples. He encouraged children to be around Him. He even said that unless you become like a child you can't see the Kingdom of God. He asked God to forgive those who had beaten Him and crucified Him.

Jesus was stating a truth about your life as a Christian. Always, always have a servant attitude and serve others. This is especially true when your own desires are tempting you to think only of yourself. Instead, be a servant to all.

46

YOUR LIFE
WHAT WILL YOUR ATTITUDE BE?

Let this mind (Attitude) be in you which was also in Christ Jesus, [6] who, being in the form of God, did not consider it robbery to be equal with God, [7] but made Himself of no reputation, taking the form of a bondservant, and coming in the likeness of men. [8] And being found in appearance as a man, He humbled Himself and became obedient to the point of death, even the death of the cross.

—PHILIPPIANS 2:5-8

ON EASTER SUNDAY, SOME OF the world will come to your church building and watch the church (you and me) worship God. The world will dress in their Easter best as if they do this every week, and what will our attitude be toward them? The world will seek out the closest parking places in a crowded parking lot and park in it as if they paid for the spot, and what will our attitude be toward them?

The world will sit where the sound is best, the air is best, the lighting is best and closest to the door for a quick escape, as if they paid for the chair in which they sit. They may even complain that the chair is too hard, too soft or too close to the next chair, and what will our attitude be toward them? The world will want a worship guide, full-color, original content, no typos, easy to read, comprehensive in its content, brief enough to scan in seconds, full weekly calendar, and what will our attitude be toward them?

The world will expect first class music, the definition of which is: the songs that they like, sung by the people that they like, performed in a manner that makes it easy for them to hum along without straining their voice. They will expect a sound system that is neither too soft nor too loud, and what will our attitude be? The world will expect a worship hour (shorter is preferred) that is somehow inspiring without demanding action, encouraging without demanding introspection, motivational without expecting sacrifice and memorable enough to suffice until December, and what will our attitude be toward them?

The world will watch us and yet they will not want us to watch them. They will want us to meet their needs, and yet they will not want anyone to know they had needs to be met. And I ask again, what will your attitude be?

> Let this mind (Attitude) be in you which was also in Christ Jesus, ⁶ who, being in the form of God, did not consider it robbery to be equal with God, ⁷ but made Himself of no reputation, taking the form of a bondservant, and coming in the likeness of men. ⁸ And being found in appearance as a man, He humbled Himself and became obedient to the point of death, even the death of the cross.
>
> —Phil 2:5-8 (NKJV)

Therefore, let us not worry about our reputation or personal feelings, let us serve the world as bondservants. Let us be all things to all people, and let us do this with all humility, even to the point of the world running over us as they did our Lord. Our prayer should be that all people will be drawn to our Lord and find the peace that enables us to be the church in the midst of a world that doesn't know Him.

47

KNOWLEDGE
KNOWING GOD

You were shown these things so that you might know that
the LORD is God; besides him there is no other.

—DEUTERONOMY 4:35

IF YOU HAVE SEEN EITHER *The Ten Commandments* or *The Prince of Egypt*,
you have seen Hollywood try to depict God as a pillar of fire or a cloud
or mist. These movies tell the story of how the Hebrews were delivered
from slavery and left Egypt. Think about 400 years of slavery for a group
of people who were called "my people" by God Himself. For 400 years,
all the Hebrews knew about God was what was handed down orally from
one generation to the next: God the Creator and God of their fathers
Abraham, Isaac, Jacob and Joseph. They were asked to believe what was
told about God.

Then Moses, who had personally met the God that they had only heard
about, entered their lives. When Moses arrived, these people began to
experience the "things" of God. Instead of something in the past, they saw
the here and now "things" of God. God desired that, from these "things,"
the people would get to know Him.

And now, how does this verse apply for you today? This verse says
that to get to know God, He will show you "things" in your life. Is your
knowledge of God limited to what people have told you about God?
Or, just like the Hebrews, has God shown you "things" in your life that

are experiences in the here and now. I believe that God is at work in every person and situation so that someone may get to know Him. These "things" are called revelations. God revealed who He is.

He does the same to you as He did to the Hebrews. Our knowledge of Him should include our own life experiences through which He tells us more about Himself. Pay careful attention to God's unique, individual, and personal work in your life so that you will come to KNOW HIM.

God reveals Himself to you in so many ways. It takes a spiritual perspective that is provided by the Holy Spirit to recognize the revelation from God. The Bible says that a person comes to God by the leading of the Holy Spirit. Look back over your life to see if you can recognize when God revealed Himself to you and you did not realize it at the time. He does this constantly and continually. He is in the "here and now" and not the "out yonder and past."

48

GOD

HE IS IN CONTROL FOR THE SOLE
PURPOSE OF RELATIONSHIPS WITH MAN

> LORD, I have heard of your fame; I stand in awe of your
> deeds, O LORD. Renew them in our day, in our time
> make them known; in wrath remember mercy.
>
> —HABAKKUK 3:2

THIS VERSE CAN FIT ALMOST any time that man has lived. We hear about the Lord and His power. The more we learn of the Lord, the more we stand in awe of what He can do. If you were like me, before I was 30, I could not tell you the "fame" of the Lord. I was Biblically ignorant even though I accepted Christ when I was 12. I wasted 18 years of not getting to know the deeds of the Lord. That's a shame.

The verse above also alludes to the fact that not many people at the time knew of the Lord. Habakkuk is asking God for a renewal of who He is to His people (in our case, Believers or Christians). If you walked into church next week and were handed a test on modern news, how would you do? If you were handed a test on the deeds of the Lord, could you clearly identify what God has done in the world and in your life? I don't think many of us would pass.

Habakkuk asked God to make known His deeds in our time. I think we are at the same time in history. God will make known His deeds, but will we be able to understand them and apply them to our lives? You see, His deeds are spiritual in nature. For example, we all know about the ten plagues of Egypt and how devastating they were. God had asked Pharaoh to let His people go. We can become enamored with the plagues that were physical manifestations of God's spiritual purpose. Read about the plagues (Exodus); they are some of the most fantastic deeds of our God.

And, if you read carefully, you'll notice that the Israelites and the Egyptians were placed in the position that they found themselves, so that they would come to know the Lord. I find this amazing, and I know God applies the same principle today. In other words, worldly events occur so that people will get to know God.

God was releasing the Hebrews from their slavery, but that wasn't God's main objective. His purpose, if you read carefully, was for the Egyptians to get to know Him. Even with the plagues, God demonstrated control over Egyptian gods, because each plague was directed at one of their gods.

If you think about world events today (and there's a lot of them), God's purpose in all these events is for people to get to know Him. Instead of focusing on the worldly event that is occurring, God wants us to see Him at work. And, when you see Him at work, you want to stand in awe and know that God is in control of this world and everything that happens to it. He has a purpose, and that is to have a strong healthy relationship with every man, woman, and child. I am amazed at His entering the three dimensional world to cause things to happen so that we can shout, "Glory Hallelujah! Our God is at work to bring people to Him!"

As you continue to live your life, the more you focus on God's deeds and His purpose, the events of this world become very incidental. God has granted you peace that passes all understanding, because you are focused on the spiritual aspect of your life. Free yourself up with a strong relationship with God and not with this world. It's your choice.

49

YOUR LIFE
THE IMPORTANCE OF "US"

Let us draw near to God with a sincere heart in full assurance of faith.

—HEBREWS 10:22A

THE "US" IN THIS VERSE is me and you and all other Believers. Do you look forward to meeting with other Believers, mixing it up with other people? Or, is your "religion" so personal that you do not think that "drawing near to God" can include others?

Fellowship with other Believers was extremely important in the early church, and I think it is even more important today. It is so easy to get "lost" in church when there is no fellowship. We need each other to draw closer to God, because we can discuss our love and worship of God. At the same time, we can grow to depend on each other when we are hurting or in need. If you do not spend time with other Believers, your spiritual compass can go haywire. We need each other to stay on the right path toward truth. This can happen only through fellowship.

Our fellowship should not be just food and gossip, but should always include moments of worship of God among a group of people. We should not leave God out of our fellowship, and we should not leave each other alone to grow in our faith. I have seen a body of Believers without fellowship and the sight is not very pretty. Usually cliques develop so that new people cannot feel welcomed. Gossip runs rampant, because the truth is not made known in a group of people. The truth is compromised, because no one gets together and stands up and reminds others of what God's truth is according to His Word.

When you add "with a sincere heart in full assurance of faith," we have to be extremely cautious not to take advantage of other Believers for worldly gain. Our hearts and our faith should be directed toward God and not toward any worldly programs within our fellowship.

Another aspect of the verse above is that individualism is the greatest problem for Believers today. We have accepted the worldly philosophy of "you're number one" to the point that everything about "my religion, my faith, and my beliefs" is about what "I" believe. All of this becomes what we think is the truth about living a life for Christ.

May I say, the Bible contains TRUTH whether you believe it or not. Jesus is the TRUTH whether you think it or not. God is all about the TRUTH whether your religion practices it or not. The TRUTH about Christianity is the giving up of self to love God and serve others. Is this your religion? If your Christianity is all about the way "you" want to grow as a Christian, is this the TRUTH? Spend some "quality time" with the Holy Spirit asking what your religion is and what the TRUTH is.

As a result, start looking for opportunities to fellowship with others that include a spiritual emphasis. It's during these times that you will see the needs of others and respond to those needs. You will be closer to the TRUTH than you have ever been before.

50

DISCIPLE

WHAT YOU SHOULD BE

WORKING ON!

In the same way, any of you who does not give up
everything he has cannot be my disciple.

—LUKE 14:33

THIS VERSE IS DEFINITELY ONE that is a tough saying of Jesus. Most of
you may want to stop reading now, because this will convict you if
you think you are a good Christian. It will turn you inside out about how
you handle money and being a disciple of Christ.

"Disciple" is rarely used as a modern term. At one time, whenever I
heard the word, *disciple*, I would think of a hooded monk in a monastery.
That sort of fits the verse above because it describes someone who has given
up worldly possessions to go off and live a life of solitude. What would you
think if someone referred to you as a "disciple"? Would it be a compliment
or a snide remark? May I suggest that you as a Believer should want to be
called a "disciple" of Christ and not be ashamed of it.

When Jesus said to give up everything, He did not mean to live the
monastic life. During His ministry on earth, there were people who "had"
things that supported His ministry. Although these people may have been
rich by worldly standards, they were being disciples when they would say,
"I don't own anything; God owns it all and He can use it in anyway He

wants." May I say that the first step toward discipleship is to consider that you have nothing other than what God has loaned you to use for His glory. Therefore, a disciple is someone who is giving up everything that God has given him/her to help others grow closer to God.

This is a tremendous life attitude and life commitment verse. Jesus intended to change the hearts and minds of Believers. It is so easy to adopt the worldly attitude that your paycheck is yours. You want to buy things with it. May I suggest that it is at this point that you behave as a disciple or not. How about your attitude and commitment? Here is the heart of the matter concerning how you handle money: after you have tithed to the church, you want to put some money aside to help others. What most of us do is spend above our income and are therefore continuously paying off debt. There is no opportunity to share with others in need.

We can never reach the ideal of being a disciple of Christ by the definition that Jesus gave in this verse. All Believers should have resources that are available to help others. What resources do you have? Money is probably not one of them, because you have adopted the worldly attitude toward spending. This is why the Christian life should be one of constant change in the way we think and in our value system. We should be convicted of worldly thinking and replace it with spiritual truths.

Another way of putting it is this: a disciple is one learning to live their life as Jesus would. The mission that God gave Jesus was to give up everything (including His own life) so that we could have a relationship with God. As disciples, we "give up" so that others can see God.

If this verse and my explanation of it hit you hard, it is the Holy Spirit. Only the Holy Spirit can provide you with the power to change your attitude and commitment. But, do you want to change or do you love your worldly possessions? Every Christian should be involved in helping others. It is the heart of discipleship. And, you should be doing something every day to grow in being a disciple of Christ!

51

YOUR LIFE

YOUR VALUE AS A BELIEVER

Man does not see what the LORD sees, for man sees what is visible, but the LORD sees the heart.

—1 SAMUEL 16:7B

Jesus said, "Stop judging by mere appearances, and make a right judgment."

—JOHN 7:24

MANY PEOPLE BELIEVE, AND YOU may think this also, that your value as a human being is determined by how you measure up to the value of things of this world: houses, cars, job title, golf score, clothes, purses, performance evaluations, grades, behavior of your children, etc., etc. All of the things in the world are judged by their outward "appearance" and a value is attached to each one. May I say that all of us accept the philosophy of the world that the value of a person is determined by their appearance? This is something that all Believers struggle with, and it is probably one of the most devastating aspects to a Believer in living their life for God.

Our challenge is to accept people the way God accepts people: He loves everyone; He died for everyone; He desires that none be separated from Him. So, He looks on the inside at their heart, not their outward appearance, actions, or behavior. But, what about their "heart"? No one knows their heart except them and God. What kind of heart is it? Everyone as a child had a tender heart (even 4th grade boys!). What happens to our hearts?

Everyone's heart gets ripped up one side and down the other because of the world. Others tell us (by the way they treat us) how smart or dumb we are, how big or small we are, how rich or poor we are. But God loves you just the way you are! That is where a Believer obtains true value – an eternal value from God and not this world.

Don't seek or accept your value based on this world. You have a relationship with God that is based on the death and resurrection of Jesus Christ and not what you are like on the outside. This truth is life-giving! It frees you up from trying to meet specific goals or live by certain criteria that others throw at you. Live today in light of God's unconditional, sacrificial, life-giving, bondage-breaking, full and complete LOVE! You are that valuable! Now, go and help others see an abundant life made possible by God through His Son, Jesus Christ.

52

ETERNITY
YOU HAVE TO DECIDE
THERE IS NO GOD

He has made everything beautiful in its time. He has also
set eternity in the hearts of men; yet they cannot fathom
what God has done from beginning to end.

—ECCLESIASTES 3:11

WOW!! THIS IS AN UNBELIEVABLE statement about God. He has made
everything and everything will be beautiful in its time. For people,
He has created a new spiritual being in each Believer that will be made
"like Him" in heaven. Instead of climbing Mt Everest, a Believer will
descend to the top of Mt. Everest. For the earth, He will, one day, make a
new earth that will be unbelievably beautiful. Think of a grander Grand
Canyon or a larger Niagara Falls. Can you imagine this?

But even more amazing about the above verse is that He has put the
reality of "eternity" into everyone. I take this to mean that every single
living human being has inside of them the yearning and potential to know
God. It takes a decision by a person NOT to believe there is a God. It's
like what God put into migrating birds and animals. Somehow, by God's
design, these birds and animals have an internal clock and GPS system that
motivates them to move at a precise time of the year and to a particular
location that may be thousands of miles away. WOW!!!

But, when God planted the idea of Him inside of us, unlike the migrating birds and animals, He gave man the opportunity to decide to migrate toward Him or away from Him. And, the further people remove God from their lives the more they cannot "fathom" that there is a God. And, just like any bird or animal that does not migrate will be in trouble, a person will face all kinds of troubles in living a life without God.

Do you live each day in the amazing wonderment of what God has done and will do? Such a perspective will definitely change the way you live your life. Migrate toward the One that put eternity into your heart! You have to decide God is already in everyone's life. If you do not accept Christ, then you are announcing to everyone that there is no God! When you accept Christ, you are affirming the TRUTH of God's love for you.

CONCLUSION

In *LIFE-CHANGING VERSES VOLUME 2*, I have provided Christians with a unique "devotional" book. However, I do not want it referred to as a devotional book due to its emphasis on real and practical application of God's Word to the lives of Christians. It's a book about, "What is a real Christian?"

I also hope that Believers who read *Life-Changing Verses Volume 2* will be encouraged to read and study their Bible more in-depth. I know this is probably not the case with most Bible scholars, but I think that God's story is in every verse of the Bible. I know some verses would be really tough to see God's story, but I believe it is possible. This makes God's Word so exciting to realize that He provided the words that we read in the Bible, and every verse has something to say to us.

I have written almost 200 *Life-Changing Verses*. 52 of those are in this Volume 2. Volume 3 is planned to be published in November, 2013 with another 52 chapters. Volume 4 is planned for sometime in 2014. Based on the success or failure of these books, I plan to write a *Life-Changing Verses* for Men and a *Life-Changing Verses* for Parents. I welcome any other specific groups that may fit into the context of *Life-Changing Verses*. Please email me with your suggestions.

After teaching through the Bible 7 times over 14 years, God has given me a perspective of His spiritual realm and Satan's current rule over the earth. I will leave you with the knowledge that Satan's rule is on borrowed time. Jesus will return and everything will change to God's glory and His purpose.

As Paul said in his letters, he wanted to go on to be with the Lord (i.e., die), but God had plans for him on this earth. I too want to go on to be with the Lord, and I have told Him so. But, that is up to Him and in the mean time, I grow more and more excited each day realizing that we are one day closer to seeing Christ appear.

My writings reflect this kind of thinking, because I believe God's Word as the ultimate and authoritative TRUTH about life. When talking with others, it is easy to identify Christians who have not made the Second Coming of Christ a part of the way they live. I think they are missing God's blessing that He gave us from Genesis through Revelation.

I encourage you to let me know your true thoughts about this volume. Let me know your favorite ones and the ones that you felt conviction from the Holy Spirit. I also invite you to ask any questions that you may have about the Bible. Send them to me at carltonlcv@gmail.com.

LIST OF BIBLE VERSES USED

OLD TESTAMENT		NEW TESTAMENT	
Genesis 11:8-9	39	Matthew 5:8	18
Deuteronomy 29:29	13	Matthew 16:12	23
Deuteronomy 4:35	47	Mark 6:5-6	5
1 Samuel 16:7b	51	Mark 9:35	45
2 Chronicles 20:9	36	Mark 12:29-31	34
Ezra 7:9b-10	11	Luke 7:9	12
Esther 4:14	8	Luke 9:46-48	16
Job 1:8	4	Luke 14:33	50
Psalm 27:1	37	John 7:24	51
Psalm 51:11-12	24	John 16:14	38
Psalm 139:14	28	Acts 4:13	15
Ecclesiastes 3:11	52	Acts 14:16-17	25
Ecclesiastes 5:1-2	42	Acts 17:11	35
Jeremiah 1:6-8	21	Acts 17:26-28	1
Jeremiah 29:11	30	Romans 2:16	46
Daniel 2:19-22	27	Romans 6:13	17
Daniel 4:35	20	Romans 8:9	6
Habakkuk 3:2	48	Galatians 4:9	2
Haggai 1:2-4	26	Ephesians 5:1-2	43
Haggai 1:5-7	41	Ephesians 5:8-10	14
		Philippians 1:6	22
		Philippians 2:5-8	3
		Philippians 3:8-9	40
		Titus 2:11-14	29
		Hebrews 4:12	44
		Hebrews 10:22	19
		James 1:5	49
		1 Peter 1:8	31
		1 Peter 4:10-11	7
		1 Peter 5:7	33
		1 John 2:15-17	32
		Revelation 22:20-21	9,10

INDEX OF MAJOR TOPICS

God	27	He is active in today's world events	Daniel 2:19-22
God	32	Cares for you	1 Peter 5:7
God	39	Always does what is best for you	Genesis 11:8-9
God	48	He is in control for the sole purpose of relationships with man	Habakkuk 3:2
God	1	Is not an impersonal God!	Acts 17:26-28
God	8	Has prepared you for divine encounters	Esther 4:14
Grace	44	What it does for us	Titus 2:11-14
Holy Spirit	24	Your guarantee from God	Psalm 51:11-12
Holy Spirit	38	Brings glory to Christ	John 16:14
Jesus	15	Boldness from knowing Him	Acts 4:13
Jesus	17	He came once and He's coming again!	Revelation 22:20-21
Jesus Christ	5	How do you see him?	Mark 6:5-6
Knowledge	47	Knowing God	Deuteronomy 4:35
Love	9	The World or the love of God? – Part 1	1 John 2:15-17
Love	10	The World or the love of God? – Part 2	1 John 2:15-17
The Bible	35	A Book to Read	Acts 17:11

Wisdom	31	Comes from God	James 1:5
You	26	Are the temple of the Holy Spirit	Haggai 1:2-4
You	28	Are created special by God	Psalm 139:14
Your Life	2	Offer yourself continually to God	Romans 6:13
Your Life	3	Should be light	Ephesians 5:8-10
Your life	4	Whatever it takes!	Job 1:8
Your life	7	Filled with inexpressible joy	1 Peter 1:8
Your life	14	Staying on course	Galatians 4:9
Your life	16	A wake-up call in serving others	Luke 9:46-48
Your life	21	God's Feet and Mouth	Jeremiah 1:6-7
Your life	22	Imitate God?	Ephesians 5:1-2
Your life	23	Guard your mind	Matthew 16:12
Your life	29	Focused on Christ	Philippians 3:8-9
Your life	30	God has a plan	Jeremiah 29:11
Your life	33	Spiritual Gift	1 Peter 4:10-11
Your life	34	Correct obedience	Mark 12:29-31
Your Life	36	What to do when times are tough	2 Chronicles 20:9

Your Life	37	What are you afraid of?	Psalm 27:1
Your life	40	Growing Christ-like	Philippians 1:6
Your life	43	Who is in control?	Romans 8:9
Your Life	45	Are you first or last?	Mark 9:35
Your Life	46	What will your attitude be?	Philippians 2:5-8
Your life	49	Importance of "US"	Hebrews 10:22
Your life	51	Your value as a Believer	John 7:24
Your Life	51	Your value as a Believer	1 Samuel 16:7b
Your Thoughts	41	Pay attention to what you are thinking	Haggai 1:5-7

ACKNOWLEDGEMENTS

I APPRECIATE WEST BOW PRESS and Thomas Nelson for the opportunity to publish *Life-Changing Verses – Volume 2.*

The staff and people of First Baptist Church, Cumming, GA have truly lived up to the "church that gives itself away." Over the years, they have supported *Life-Changing Verses* and given constant feedback and encouragement to me.

Of particular note is Dr. Lou Meier who, on many long walks, discussed and debated the weekly *Life-Changing Verses*. Dr. Meier was also instrumental in encouraging me to publish *Life-Changing Verses Vol 1.*

My family has always been supportive throughout this work, and I thank them for their encouragement..

My other daughter (in-law), Ginger, did yeoman's work in reviewing, editing, and correcting the numerous errors I made in the final draft. Her work was instrumental in finalizing a clean edited copy of the manuscript. I am indebted to her for her investment in this book and her belief that God has called me to write these books.

And, finally, my wife (D'Ette) of 43 years has been there throughout this project. She was involved in reading, reviewing, and offering constructive suggestions. Her diligence was amazing to me as she read and reread copies of the manuscripts. Her encouragement was very much needed at times of fatigue and my questioning the value of these books. She has met my every need.

ABOUT THE AUTHOR

CARLTON LEE ARNOLD HAS HAD a wide experience of teaching the Bible and reviewing numerous Christian curriculums. He served in the USAF for seven years. After retiring from Verizon in 2003, he worked five years on staff at First Baptist Church, Cumming, GA as Director of Adult Discipleship.

He and his wife have lived in Georgia, Texas, Alabama, Missouri, Florida, and New York which has given them a wide perspective of different churches.

He now lives with his family in close proximity in the Cumming, GA area.

Any comments or suggestions can be sent to carltonlcv@gmail.com.

INDEX

CPSIA information can be obtained at www.ICGtesting.com
Printed in the USA
LVOW050350150513

333750LV00002B/125/P